ISBN-13: 978-0-578-84705-4

Cover design by: Art Painter
Library of Congress Control Number: 2018675309
Printed in the United States of America

CONTENTS

Preface

I had been working in the embedded systems for thirty plus years. In those years, I had seen the evolution of the industry from primitive 8-bit microprocessors to 32-bit/64-bit SoC chips. The clock frequency of the processor was 1MHz back in 1980s. Now the clock frequency can reach 1 GHz. And the 64 Kbyte memory was luxury at that time. Nowadays, memory is in the multiple Mbytes. Also, hardware and software tools have improved dramatically since then. Without the modern tools, it is nearly impossible to design and develop an embedded system.

During my career, I had worked on the medical imaging, such as CT imaging and Ultrasound imaging, the CDMA handset, the wireless communications, and the avionics navigation systems. After all these years' experience, I have an urge to pass my knowledge to the engineers and the students who are interested in the embedded system or who are new to this field.

This book starts with the definition of the embedded system in Chapter 1. Chapter 2 defines the scope of the book. It is very difficult to cover the whole embedded system in one place.

Chapter 3 emphases the importance of the embedded system life cycle. Beyond the regulatory industries, such as medical systems, avionics systems or hazardous industry, the process control is often ignored. This chapter describes the components in each phase, and how to assure the quality of the product.

Chapter 4 and 5 describe the evolution of microprocessor/microcontroller and DSP which starts with a simple CPU core, and became an SoC. The CPU core includes Arithmetic Logic Unit (ALU), sequencer and core registers. Inside the processor/DSP, there are core peripherals, such as NVIC (Nested Vector Interrupt Controller), Cache, SIU (System Interface Unit), Clock Synthesizer, Timers, DMA Controller (Direct Memory Access Controller) ...etc.

In addition to the core peripherals, the processor/DSP has peripherals to communicate with the devices outside the processor/DSP. In Chapter 6, those peripherals include SPI (Serial Peripheral Interface), I2C/I^{2}C (Inter-Integrated Circuit), UART (Universal Asynchronized Receiver and Transmitter), Ethernet,

USB (Universal Serial Bus), …etc. This chapter also explains how the Cyclic Redundancy Check (CRC) works.

How to choose a processor/DSP is an important process. Usually, an embedded product has many requirements to implement, but there is only a limited target budget and time to complete the product. How to make balance between the requirements and the time/budget requires some thoughts. Chapter 7 lists some thoughts to choose a processor/DSP.

Chapter 8 talks about the difference between Big-Endian and Little-Endian, and how the orders of the bytes are stored in the memory. I have seen a hardware engineer who mixed up with the endian. End up the board was modified with bunch of wires to correct the error.

Nowadays memory is much cheaper, but for the embedded product, memory size is limited. The choice of memory becomes important. Chapter 9 introduces different types of memory. Which type(s) of memory fits the product best requires careful selection.

In the real-time world, interrupts are essential. Without interrupts, it is very difficult to handle the timing critical events. Chapter 10 illustrates how the nested interrupts work.

For some embedded products, there is no end-user to reset the system. When something goes wrong in the system, the system requires a reset. It relies on the watchdog to accomplish the job. Chapter 11 describes how the watchdog timer works.

Chapter 12 talks briefly about the hardware prototype boards. To gain some confidence before the massive production, hardware prototype boards can provide some peace of mind for the hardware engineers.

As the requirements grows, software can become complicated. During the design phase, it is important to partition software into smaller components. So, it is easier to implement, debug and test those components. Software components can be easily kept in isolation. So, breaking software into small components has the security benefits. Chapter 13 describes the software components.

When the software requirements need to handle critical events, and the number of software components increases, Real-time OS (RTOS) can help software design to sort out the complexity, and to meet the requirements. Chapter 14 describes the difference between the Bare Metal System and Real-time OS, and the concept of physical addressing and virtual addressing. It also talks about the benefits and drawbacks of using the Real-time OS.

Chapter 15 discusses the software tools, such as the Integrated Development Environment (IDE) which are essential to develop software for the modern processors/DSP. Those tools help the software developers to write the code, to compile and link the code, to download the code to the target, and to debug the code on the target.

Writing code is not difficult, but to prove that the code meets the requirements, and that the code is bug free, needs careful thoughts. Chapter 16 lists some efficient skills for programming and some common mistakes in programming. It also describes the software debugging skills, the unit test, requirement traceability, and code review.

Chapter 17 describes the processor boot-up procedures. It provides with two examples of boot procedure, ARM Cortex-M, and PowerPC. It also talks the secure boot, and bootloader.

When hardware and software are complete, they need be tested to prove that they meet the requirements. Chapter 18 talks about the formal release, hardware test, software test, and system verification and validation.

Chapter 19 talks about the product maintenance. After the product is released and shipped, it doesn't mean the job is all done, especially true for the long-haul products. During the product life cycle, bug fixing and improvement will keep going as long as the product is on the market. So, maintenance is important although it is boring.

Mechanical Design is not part of the electronics design, but it should not be ignored. There are specifications for the product to meet. It may also provide the security device to protect the product. Chapter 20 lists some thoughts for the mechanical design.

Chapter 21 details the RSA Public-Key Cryptosystem which is an asymmetric cryptosystem. RSA cryptosystem is based on very large prime numbers and intensive computations. This chapter explains how the cryptosystem works, and provides the algorithms for finding the prime number, computing the Extended Euclidean Algorithm, and the Binary Powering Algorithm. The sample C code in 64-bit integer for the RSA Public-Key encryption and decryption is available for reference. This chapter also shows the algorithm of the Division of Nonnegative Integer in large arrays.

Another cryptosystem, Advanced Encryption Standard (AES), is detailed in Chapter 22. AES is a symmetric cryptosystem. It is used by the US government and private industries. This chapter talks about the features of AES, the Finite Field Computation, the generation of the Byte Substitution and the Inverse Byte Substitution Tables (the multiplicative inverse and the affine transformation), the Key Expansion, how to encrypt the message, and how to decrypt the ciphered message. The sample C code for encryption and decryption is available for reference.

The final chapter, Chapter 23, discusses the future of the embedded system. It includes the speed and size of the processor, the security, the connectivity for IoT, the battery life, the artificial intelligence/machine learning, and the Post-quantum Cryptography.

Here, I want to thank Dr. Paul S. Wang at Kent State University, Kent, Ohio for his guidance through the RSA Public-Key Cryptosystem. With his tireless instructions, I finished my master's thesis, "The Experimental Implementation of the RSA Public-Key Cryptosystem under UNIX".

During my embedded system career, I had a chance to work with some talent scientists and hardware engineers. I implemented the algorithms that the scientists innovated. I also wrote embedded software, such as drivers, firmware, the boot code, and the application code, for the microcontroller/DSP boards that the hardware engineers designed. Given a brand-new board, I was able to bring up the hardware and build a framework for the software. We worked together as a team to achieve the goals. Here I would like to thank my former colleagues, Dr. Heang K. Tuy, Mr. Calum Mackinnon, and Mr. Brian Sargent, for their help during my career. With Dr. Tuy and 2 other engineers, we were awarded the patent of "System to Reformat Images for Three Dimensional Display", i.e., reformatting the CT images for the 3D display that provides a better view for the radiologists.

I also want to express my thanks to Bart Van Assche, PhD, for his dedication to check the errors in the book and suggested to add AES cryptosystem to the book. Also, many thanks to my wife for her encouragement to write the book.

I have tried my best to make my writing clear. If the reader has any concern or confusion about the writing, please contact me at mbedguide@outlook.com.

Samuel HJ Lin at Morgan Hill, CA

This page intentionally left blank

1 What is an Embedded System?

An embedded system is an electronic system which is designed for certain dedicated function or functions. It can be any computer system, except PC, Workstation, or Mainframe computers which have the general purpose of usage. It is designed for special purpose.

The size of an embedded system can be as small as a digital watch. Or it can be as large as a spacecraft. But don't be deceived by the size of an embedded system. A small embedded system product can be as complicated as a large system. For example, a cellphone not only has a sophisticated hardware, it also has intricate software. The size of a cellphone is small, but it has a microprocessor, LCD for display for user interface, digital camera, microphone, speaker, digital and analog communication components, and chipsets for handling the special protocol, ... etc.

Since the embedded system is dedicated to specific functions, design engineers can optimize it to reduce the size and cost of the product, and increase the reliability and performance. It is especially true for those consumer products which have huge quantities in production. A small reduction in the cost can increase the profit a lot. In this book, we emphasize on the process control, security, and choosing the hardware and software.

In contrast to the personal computer market, the hardware is designed to fit the specific functions, and software is written specially for an application. Usually, the embedded system has limited resources, such as memory, storage, power, processing capacity, and cost. Also, unlike a commercial product that software can be installed by the end user, it is difficult to let the user to install the software to an embedded system. Embedded system software is installed in the factory by the manufacturer before the product is shipped. For the software updating in the field, it can be achieved by downloading through the internet connection, or installing the software on site by the trained personnel.

2 The Scope and the Definition of Terms

There are a lot of subjects to talk about in an embedded system. It is not possible to touch all the subjects. Here this book concentrates on the point view of an engineer or a developer, either hardware or software. So, this is not a book about theories. It is more like about the knowledge about the embedded system, what kind of problems may encounter while designing and developing an embedded system, and how to solve those problems, and what kind of technology is behind the solutions.

At the same time, the new technology for the future is also discussed. Recently IoT has widely spread into many fields of industry. Not only the technology improves with time, the security of IoT devices is getting more and more attention.

Take operating systems for example, there are so many operating systems on the market. Some are real-time, and some are not. Here only the real-time operating systems are covered. For an embedded system, real-time plays an important role to response to the environment.

Other things like microprocessors and DSP's, there are so many of those on the market. It is impractical to cover all of them. This book only talks about the 32-bit processors, such as ARM processors, NXP PowerPC, and TI TMS320C6xxx DSP.

DEFINITION OF TERMS

In the requirements, there are some terms that are used to describe the importance of the requirements. Here is the definition of terms:

- shall – It is absolutely a must.
- should – It is strongly recommended.
- guideline – It is less strong recommendation.

3 Life Cycle of an Embedded System

An embedded system product may last only a short time, such as consumer electronics. Others may last 10, 20 years or even longer, such as avionic instruments, satellites, and spacecrafts. But all products are driven by the demand of the market. When a company or an organization has decided to produce an embedded system/product, it has to figure out the demand of the product. For a company, it is expected to make profits from the product. So, the marketing department needs to find out the demand on the market, and to detail the specifications of the product.

In some other cases, the embedded product is driven from the engineering or the research department. When engineers/researchers have come up some brilliant ideas for a new product, they would persuade the marketing to introduce the new product, and get the feedback from the potential customers.

Then following the marketing specifications or its own ideas, the engineering department starts gathering design information for the product. It starts from the requirements, followed by the design, implementation, testing. The final product must meet all the customer's specifications and demands. Customers don't want a product that does not meet the specifications. The engineering department also needs to perform a comprehensive test to ensure the integrity of the final product.

Even after the product is on the market, customers may find some bugs or request changing the requirements. So, the engineering department will keep maintaining the product. Since the requirement has changed, the system also needs to perform the regression test.

Here are the major components of the embedded system's life cycle:

- Marketing Specifications/Engineering Innovation
- System Requirements
- Hardware Requirements
- Software Requirements
- System Design
- Hardware Design
- Hardware Prototype

- Hardware Test
- Software Design
- Software Development
- Software Test
- System Integration Test
- Maintenance

Those components can be divided into the following phases:

- Requirement Phase
- Design Phase
- Implementation Phase
- Integration Test Phase
- Maintenance Phase

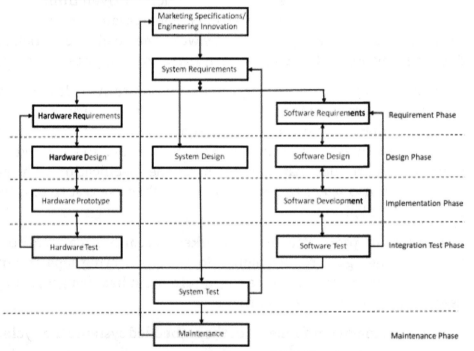

Figure 1 : Embedded System Life Cycle

This engineering process can be implemented in the Waterfall model or the Iterative and Incremental model.

- Waterfall model – In this model, the next phase can be proceeded only after the previous phase is fully developed and reviewed. It is a less flexible approach. But if the client and the engineers fully understand what the product would be, the Waterfall mode can predict how much time is needed for each phase. It is a better time control method. Also, it has better documentation. When engineers leave the company in the middle of the project, it is easier for new engineers to pick up.

- Iterative and Incremental model – Sometimes, the client and the engineers are not sure about the outcome of the design. Therefore, the engineers break the system into small portions, and develop the system portion by portion. Engineers learn from each small portion, and go back to modify the design. This model is commonly used in the design and development phases. But it is not appropriate for the requirements. Agile Project Management falls in the same category.

According to the statistics, if a bug is caught earlier, the cost to fix the bug is less. Therefore, it is important to find the bug during the development. The cost for the early fixing is minimum. If the bug is found during the integration test, the cost to fix the bug is more, and it is required to retest the whole system. Even worse when the bug is found in the field, the cost not only includes the fix and retest, it also includes the cost of sending the personnel to fix the system in the field. So, it is very important to fix the bug as earliest as possible.

For highly regulated industries, such as medical devices or aviation/avionics products, process control is a must for controlling the quality. In USA, FAA has DO-178B/C guidance for airborne software. In DO-178B/C, Software Life Cycle is a critical section. The Life Cycle section includes:

- Defining Requirements
- Software Designing
- Coding Development
- Integrating Test

3.1 Requirement Phase

Before attempting to start designing and implementing of a product, engineers need to sit down and discuss what are the requirements of the product, i.e., what kind of functions the product should provide. This process may not be as exciting as other phases, but it is essential to make the product successful.

Requirements can be treated as goals. They describe the functionality and non-functionality of the product. It is just like setting the goals of the product. What kind of expectation the product should become? What kind of the behaviors it should be?

All requirements have to comply with the government regulations and to meet the industry's standards. Each requirement must be clearly defined and very specific. It must not be ambiguous or broadly defined. Since it is clearly defined, it helps the design, implementation, testing, and verifying in the future.

3 .1.1 Marketing Specifications/Engineering Innovation

Marketing collects information from the customers, and decides what kind of product can be sold in the market, such as cameras, cellphones … etc. Or the marketing gets the requests from the customers to build a specific product for them, such as the navigation system, or the radar system used by the airplane. The marketing creates a new product plan which specifies functions of the product in high-level form. It describes what the product should look like and behave.

3.1.2 System Requirements

The system group transforms the marketing specifications into requirements which specify in detail how the product behaves, such as the timing requirements, functional requirements, design constraints, and user interface if any. The system requirements generalize the definition that needs be met in designing a system or sub-system. Remember the requirement describes what the product is, not how the product works.

Each individual system requirement must be clear. It shall have at least a derived requirement in the hardware requirement and the software requirement. From the system requirements, each individual requirement shall be able to trace down to at least one hardware requirement and software requirement, and vice versa. The traceability is bi-directional.

System requirements may affect the hardware selection and the software selection, especially the RTOS. For example, there is a system requirement such as all data need be encrypted during transmitting. This kind of requirement would affect the choice of the microcontroller that has the encryption function hardware. Another example is if the system requirement that the received data need be processed in a certain time constraint, then software needs to select a RTOS that can meet the requirement.

The more thorough the requirements are, the better the product will be. But we are talking about the achievable requirements, not those requirements that are beyond the current technology. So, the requirements must be carefully reviewed by all counterparts, such as system engineers, hardware engineers, software engineers, and test engineers.

Remember, system requirements are just like goal setting. They are the goals for the product. They describe what need be achieved for the product. Without the requirements, it is hard to make a sound product.

3.1.2.1 Security Requirements

Security of the embedded system is becoming an important topic, especially in the IoT field. It is a necessary measure to protect the product. Attacks may come in any kind of formality. According to the statistics, in current days 95% of the attacks comes from network. Only 5% is the physical attacks. The attacks include:

- Attacks from network – These attacks include gathering the sensitive information, tampering the firmware, downloading unauthorized code, intercepting of transmitting packages, injecting the false packages, or causing the stack overflow.
- Physical attacks – These attacks happen when the hacker is close to the device. There are many forms of physical attacks, such as changing the temperature, voltage, or frequency to make the system fail. Some attacks may use Side Channel Analysis (SCA) to steal the keys which is stored in IoT device.

Security becomes a must, not an option any more. Designers have to look into the security issues at the beginning of designing a product, not in the middle or at the end of the product cycle. Therefore, to implement the security issues has to start from requirements.

First, the designers need to identify the data assets that need be protected, and the threats that come from what kinds of the attack. After identifying the data assets and the threats, the designers can create requirements for protecting the assets and guarding against the attacks. To protect the data assets, it can be classified into three categories (the famous CIA in the security industry):

- Confidentiality – Keeping data assets secret and private. Only the authorized party can access the data assets. Hackers won't be able to access the data.
- Integrity – Keeping the data assets from being tampered by hackers, such as boot code, device configuration data, firmware, … etc.
- Authenticity – Only the trusted parties are allowed to update the data assets, such as configuration data, firmware, … etc. They are guarded with the keys for updating.

3 .1.2.2 Ultrasound Imaging System Example

An ultrasound imaging system contains a probe, the front-end subsystem, the back-end subsystem, and the embedded control subsystem (see Figure 2: Ultrasound Imaging System). There are a lot of requirements. Usually, the patient's ultrasound images are shared with other departments in the hospital. So, after scanning, the ultrasound image will be transferred to the central database. Here is a very simple example of the requirements in the embedded control subsystem:

"The patient's ultrasound images shall be securely transferred to the remote database."

After further analyzing, the above statement contains 2 requirements: image transfer and security. Hardware and software need to address these requirements separately. From this system requirement can trace down to the related hardware requirements (see section 3.1.3.2) and software requirements (see section 3.1.4.2).

3 .1.3 Hardware Requirements

Derived from the system requirements, hardware requirements describe what need be done in hardware to meet the system requirements, such as

- Processing Speed – How fast the CPU can run? How many MIPS or MFLOPS the CPU can achieve? Speed may not completely rely on the system clock rate, or bus speed. There are some factors that can affect the processing power of the CPU, such as the wait states in accessing memory, and cache usages.
- Memory – How much RAM and flash memory are needed? If Operating System is used, how much more memory is needed?
- Timing Analysis – To ensure the whole system meets the timing requirements.
- Peripherals – Peripherals, such as Ethernet, USB, UART, SPI, I2C, allow the processor to communicate with other devices, such as temperature sensors, GPS Systems … etc.
- Power Supply – Calculate the power consumption for all devices. The total power consumption shall not exceed the power consumption stated in the system requirement.
- Memory Management Unit (MMU) – If the operating system is required, does the RTOS need an MMU in the microcontroller to perform the translation between the virtual address and the physical address?

Each hardware requirement must be able to trace back an individual system requirement, and each hardware related system requirement shall have at least a hardware requirement derived from it.

3 .1.3.1 Security Requirements

Hardware shall provide the device(s) to protect the data confidentiality, integrity, and authenticity. Also, it shall provide a secure executing environment.

3 .1.3.2 Ultrasound Imaging System Example

From the system requirement in section 3.1.2.2, hardware requirements must have:

- "An Ethernet connection shall be used to transfer the images."
- "Cryptographic accelerators shall be used for the encryption of the

image."

And in hardware design, there are low-level requirements that can trace up to these hardware requirements (see section 3.2.3.3).

3 .1.4 Software Requirements

Same as hardware requirements, software requirements are derived from system requirements. Software Requirements Specification (SRS) is a description of a software system to be developed. It lays out functional and non-functional requirements, and may include a set of use cases that describe the user interaction that the software must provide. These requirements include:

- Overall Software Description – Describe the features, functionalities, non-functionalities, objectives of the software for the whole system.
- Functional requirements on different modes – Describe how the software functions under each mode.
- User Interfaces – Describe how the user interacts with the system.
- Hardware interfaces – Drivers/firmware are provided for the interface to the hardware.
- Software Interfaces – Define the interface between the software components. What communication mechanism is used between the components?
- Performance criteria – The process to measure the software performance to determine software meets the system requirements.
- Timing requirements – Describes the time from an event occurring to software taking action, and how much time the software takes to complete the event.
- Reliability – Software is solid and bug free.
- Reusability – Make the component usable for another project.
- Portability – The developed code can be used for other platforms.
- Design Constraints – Define the restrictions of technology or resources.

Since software requirements are derived from the system requirements, for each requirement in the system requirements, there is at least one software requirement derived from it. Software may have several requirements that are derived from the same system requirement. All the software requirements shall be able to trace back to system requirements. Sometimes, Software Requirements are referred as High-Level Software Requirements.

3 .1.4.1 Security Requirements

Software shall be separated into the secure partition and non-secure partition. Critical sections of software shall be executed in a secure environment. Software shall ensure the integrity of the data while transferring, and protect the data from tampering, or protect the code from the accessing or updating by the unauthorized parties.

3 .1.4.2 Ultrasound Imaging System Example

From the system requirement (see section 3.1.2.2), there are at least 2 requirements in this statement. So, software requirements must have:

- "Ultrasound images shall be packed into Ethernet frames/packets for transfer." (see Figure 24: Ethernet Frame/Packet Structure)
- "The Ethernet payload data in the frames/packets shall be encrypted before transfer."

In software design, there are low-level requirements that can trace up to these software requirements (see section 3.2.4.2).

3 .1.4.3 Coding Standard

A clean and readable code can help engineers to debug and maintain the code in the future. Engineers usually won't stay on the same project forever. The original author may move to different project, and a new person takes over the code. If the code is written in a neat and organized style, the new person can easily understand the code.

Engineers don't like to be constrained or confined. But in order to keep every person in the same page, some rules are required. In the C/C++ coding standard, here are serval examples of requirements that need be addressed:

- Filename in the file header.
- Company name and copy right in the file header.
- Description of the functions in the file header.
- Modified date and comments in the file header.
- Proper indent for each line.
- Alignment of "{" and "}" in the same column.
- Comments for each routine.
- Only one statement in each line.
- The security concerns.

Since C and C++ are popular in the embedded system, Software Engineering

Institute (SEI) has created "CERT C" for coding standard. Also, Motor Industry Software Reliability Association (MISRA) produces guidelines for the software development in the automotive industry. Both "CERT C" and "MISRA C" have very good resources for secure coding standards.

3 .2 Design Phase

After the boring Requirement Phase, engineers are eager to jump into designing the product. But don't ignore the requirements which would guide the engineers to a successful product. Without the requirements, engineers may get confused or wonder into the wrong directions.

Design describes how to reach the goals. It first analyzes each requirement, and provides the solution to the requirement. It also paves the path for the implementation.

3 .2.1 Design for Test

As the technology advances, the chip is getting smaller and smaller and with Ball Grid Array (BGA) package, or the Surface Mount Technology (SMT) package, and the PCB boards are getting thicker and thicker. Although the BGA package can provide more pins, all the pins are underneath the chip. There is no way to probe the signals through those pins. For SMT package, to probe the signals through the pins is very dangerous because those pins are small and so close together. So, it is becoming harder and harder to debug the hardware and the software unless the test points are added during the hardware design.

It is also true for software. As software gets more and more complicated. It becomes necessary to break the code into small components. So, it is easier to implement, instrument the test code, and identify the bugs. It also helps to reorganize the code in the future.

The concept of design for test can make life easier in the development and test stages. Without planning ahead for the testing, it can get very difficult to debug the software, test the software, and prove the code meets the requirements.

3 .2.2 System Design

System design describes the system at the architecture level, the interfaces, the data flow, the control flow, and gives a clear view of how the whole system works together. It includes subsystems and their services, hardware mapping, data management, access control, global software control structure, and boundary conditions. It separates the system into subsystems. Use functional diagram to present an overview of the whole system, and describes the relationship between the functions.

Here is an example of the medical Ultrasound Imaging System which typically includes a probe, a Front-end subsystem, a Back-end Subsystem, and an Embedded Control System.

- Probe – It is also called Ultrasound Transducer which sends the sound wave pulses and receives the reflected sound wave.
- The Front-end – It generates the sound pulses for transmit, processes the reflected sound wave, converts the wave into digital data (I and Q), passes the digital I, Q data to the Back-end.
- The Back-end – It processes the reflected sound to find the distance of the tissues, tendons, vessels, or internal organs. Then converts the signal into video, and finally display the images on the monitor.
- Embedded Control System – Provides the user interface, such as keyboard, trackball, LED panel, touch panel, USB, Ethernet, or video recorder.

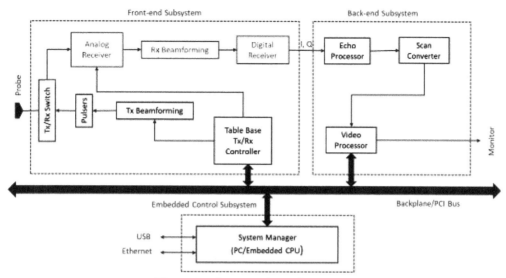

Figure 2 : Ultrasound Imaging System

3 .2.3 Hardware Design

Hardware design identifies a system's hardware components and the relations between the components. It is the architecture of the hardware, and generally includes some form of analog components, digital components, or hybrid electronic components, along with electronic and mechanical sensors and actuators. It is commonly described in the functional diagrams and the schematics. A schematic is the blueprint of the hardware architecture. It is the foundation for building and maintaining the board.

When designing the hardware, keep the testability in mind. It is not only for the hardware test; it is also for the software test. The most common practice is to leave the test points on the board. Since software sets up the registers, such as the serial clock (SCLK), MISO, MOSI signals of SPI device, it is easier for software developer to verify those signals if there are test points for them.

3 .2.3.1 Multi-board Connection

For a multi-board system, how to connect those boards together depends on the communication method between the boards: parallel communication or serial communication. Here are some schemes that are commonly used:

- For the simple system, a daughter board can piggyback on a mother board with a connector. This can be easily implemented and save the space.
- In the large system, the parallel communication, such as the old PCI/PCI-X (Peripheral Component Communication) bus, provides fast data transfer. But it requires to purchase the PCI Slots. Also, it is more complicated to design the system because to make all 32 bits work in synchronization across the boards is not an easy task. It needs each board to meet the PCI specifications. PCI bus was popular in the PC industry, but it was also used in the embedded system for data transfer between boards.
- For the serial communication, the PCI Express (PCIe) is a high-speed serial bus. It replaces the traditional parallel PCI bus.
- Ethernet is also commonly used for the inter-board communication. It is easy to add a new node, has farther distance between boards, and allows the boards to send data to each other at any time

(see section 6.5).

- For convenience, the backplane with connectors can be built in-house. The boards are situated on the connectors. The backplane is often used for the point-to-point connections, such as HDLC, UART serial communications. Each pin in the connector is assigned to a signal which is linked to the processor.

3 .2.3.2 Security

In order to ensure the confidentiality, integrity, and authenticity, hardware needs to provide the Root of Trust which is the foundation of platform for security. The hardware Root of Trust provides the following functions:

- Secure boot (see section 17.1) and secure firmware – Protecting the boot and the firmware from being tampered or stolen.
- Secure storage for keys and data – Keep the cryptographic keys and important data in a secure place. Only the authorized party can access the keys and the data.
- Trust Execution Environment (TEE) – Code can execute in the secure state or in the non-secure state, and clear the registers when switching from secure state to non-secure state. So, there is no data left for the hacker to trace.
- Secure protected memory regions – Some memory regions are protected. Only the secure code can access those regions.
- Hardware detection of stack overflow – Stack overflow is hard for software to detect it. Software can set the stack size and the region of the stack in registers. Hardware can detect the stack overflow and generate interrupts/exceptions to alert the CPU.
- Separate vector tables for the secure code and the non-secure code – In order to ensure the execution of the secure code and the non-secure code in different environments, the interrupt vector table also need be separated.
- Preventing firmware from being reverse engineered – The firmware in the flash memory or ROM needs be encrypted. The encrypted code is difficult for the hacker to perform the reverse engineering.
- Providing cryptographic functions – Although the cryptographic algorithms can be implemented in software, it takes away the CPU time, and is not as efficient as hardware executing. Hardware can accelerate the cryptographic computations.

Hardware Security Module (HSM) which includes special cryptographic accelerators, provides the engine to perform the cryptography in a fast and safe environment. It can generate the true random numbers, generate the secure cryptographic keys, perform encryption and decryption functions, and check the authentication of the sources. For more information about cryptography, please see RSA Public-Key Cryptosystems (section 21) and Advanced Encryption Standard (section 22).

The architecture of the platform security can be based on the single core or the dual-core:

- For a single core architecture, the CPU executes the code either in the secure state or in non-secure state. When switching from secure state to non-secure state, hardware shall provide a clean cut, and leave no trace of the secure information, such as the content of general-purpose registers or special registers.
- For a dual-core architecture, one processor runs the secure code and the other processor performs the non-secure code. The secure processor provides a Root-of-Trust hardware which includes hardware-accelerated cryptography, true random number generation (TRNG), and secured storage. The secure code runs on the secure processor. Also, the secure firmware services come with the Root-of-Trust hardware. The firmware includes secure boot, crypto libraries, secure storage, injecting secure assets to the device, IPC … etc. The non-secure code includes WIFI, Bluetooth, network protocol (such as MQTT), RTOS … etc.

3.2.3.3 Ultrasound Imaging System Example

From hardware requirements in section 3.1.3.2, the hardware design specifications include the following:

- "Ethernet controller shall comply with Ethernet IEEE 802.3 protocol."
- "The cryptographic accelerators shall encrypt the data before transfer."

3 .2.4 Software Design

Software design transforms the high-level software requirements into specifications which provides the blueprint for software implementation and coding. The design is considered as a two-step of process, analyzing and designing. During analyzing step, the high-level software requirement is further broken into smaller solvable elements. Then in designing step, it applies the solution to those elements. Therefore, software design is referred to "Low-Level Software Requirements", as against "High-Level" Software Requirements.

Software design also describes the software architecture which details how software is separated into components, and how the components are organized. It also describes the relationship between components and the interfaces between them, input/output definition, data and control flows, design constrains (such as memory allocation, or algorithms). A state transition diagram can help the developers to understand the whole picture.

Design for test is not only applied to hardware, it is also applied to software. How to make software be tested easily in the future is essential. "Simplicity" is the key. Tries to make design being easy to understand, and not tangled together. A good design paves the way for the implementation.

During the design process, many aspects need to be taken into consideration. Those aspects for software design may include:

- Modularity – Each component is well defined, and decoupled from each other. So, the developer can implement the component independently. The component also can be tested and validated individually. It can be easily maintained in the future.
- Portability – Port from one platform to another platform. The same software can support many platforms.
- Reusability – The component can be used in different project.
- Scalability – Software can adapt for the future expansion. If software is well defined, it is easy to add more functions in the future without much modifications.
- Testability – Each component should be able to be tested individually.
- Reliability – Software shall be able to perform the specific require-

ments.
- Security – Software shall provide a secure environment to protect the integrity of the system.

3 .2.4.1 **Security**

Software shall withstand and resist the attack from hackers. Isolation is the key to achieving security goal. Partitioning software into secure components and non-secure partitions. The partitions are isolated from each other. Only the secure Inter-Process Communication (IPC) provides the communication channel for requests between the partitions.

With the help from hardware Root-of-Trust, the safety critical components, such as boot code, firmware, configuration data, security keys, libraries, and critical code shall be kept in the secure partition. Only the secure code can access these components. The non-secure code has to call the IPC to access these components. Also, through hardware Root-of-Trust, software can check the authentication of the sources, or encrypt and decrypt the communication packets.

3 .2.4.2 **Ultrasound Imaging System Example**

The maximum size of the Ethernet payload data is 1500 bytes (see section 6.5.1). An ultrasound image is much larger than that. Therefore, the image will be broken into the payload size. Each payload contains 1500 bytes or less. The payload data is encrypted by the cryptographic accelerators. Software assembles the encrypted payload with MAC addresses and Ethernet type, then passes the frame to the Ethernet controller for transfer. From High-Level Software Requirement (see section 3.1.4.2), the Low-Level Software Requirements are:

- At initialization, Ethernet driver shall set up Ethernet related registers. (Note: if possible, specify the value of each register.)
- When an ultrasound image is ready for transfer, application code shall divide the image into the Ethernet payload data size.
- The Ethernet driver shall encrypt the payload by hardware accelerators.
- The Ethernet driver shall build the frame for transfer.
- The Ethernet driver shall set up Ethernet controller for transfer.

For these low-level software requirements, there are corresponding subroutines (see section 3.3.2.1) implemented to comply with them.

3 .3 Implementation Phase

Implementation translates the specifications and components defined in the design phase into a product or computer languages.

3 .3.1 Hardware Prototype

Hardware bug is not easy to fix after it has been built. To reduce the risk of failure, hardware engineers can build a prototype unit or units in-house to test the concept, if it is not difficult to build. Otherwise, hardware engineers can order few boards at the first spin of the board manufacturing. For some complicated system, it may take a while to get the new boards. But it is worth to wait for the boards. When the boards arrive, the hardware engineer can check out the signals to make sure they are good, the integrity of the circuit, the resistors, the capacitors, the diodes, DNS (Do Not Stuff), …etc.

3 .3.2 Software Development

Remember: Simplicity is beauty. When developing the code, make the logic straight forward, and use the language that other people can understand. Don't try to be gorgeous. Just write the code directly to the point, according to the requirements. If possible, start implementing the code from the most difficult part first. After conquering the difficult part, the developer feels more confident about the implementation. And the rest of the code is easy to implement.

When software developers start to implement the code, usually the new board is not ready. The developers can purchase the evaluation board which comes with the same processor, but the peripherals may be different. The developer can run the code on the evaluation board. So, when the real board is ready, the code can be ported to the real board.

The developer can also help the hardware engineer to test the new-spin boards. The test code is called "hardware bring-up code" which has the basic tests for the new board. It can check the memory, the peripheral devices, ... etc. The drivers and firmware of the bring-up code can evolve into the real driver code for the production. It is not waste of time.

3 .3.2.1 Ultrasound Imaging System Example

The following subroutines shall be implemented according to software design (see section 3.2.4.2):

- InitializeEthernet()
- CreatePayload()
- EncryptPayload()
- BuildFrame()
- TransferPacket()

3.4 Integration Test Phase

Integration test is the collection of all pieces of hardware and software, and conducting test as one piece. Starting from software, after each component is tested, combine all components together and perform the software integration test. When hardware test is done, then test the whole system together.

3 .4.1 Hardware Test

Hardware test is not only meant for testing the hardware to see if the hardware meets the requirements, but also undergoing abnormal conditions to see when the hardware breaks down and how it breaks. Usually, the test involves in the stress tests which include the temperature, radiation, electromagnetic Interference (EMI), humidity, lightning, … etc. tests. Hardware is placed in the abnormal environment or condition until the hardware fails to function normally. See section 18.3 for details.

3 .4.2 Software Test

The purpose of software test is to ensure the software meets the software requirements, and to root out the defects (see section 18.4 for details). It can conduct the functional testing, non-functional testing, performance testing, or regression testing. There are two approaches that software testing can be carried out:

- Black-Box Test – A Black-Box test is to treat the system as a black-box. Without knowing what is inside the software, the test engineer writes the test cases according to the requirements or specifications. The test engineer basically tests the functionalities of the product. The purpose of the Black-Box test is to see if the functions are correct or if some functions are missing. The input to the black-box can be valid data or invalid data. Then the test engineer determines the output is correct or not.

- White Box Test – In order to test the software with White-Box, the test engineer needs to understand the internal software structure and code. The main purpose of White-Box test is to trace the path through the code to check the statement coverage, branch coverage, function coverage, ... etc. According to the software requirements, the test engineer can insert the test code to a function, a branch or a statement into the source code. The test code counts how many times the function (or the branch, or the statement) has been executed. The result of the count is used to determine the code coverage of the requirements. If a piece of code is never got executed, check whether it is dead code. If it is dead code, it should be removed.

3.4.3 System Test

After all components of a system, such as hardware and software, have been fully tested and have passed the test, the system test gathers all components and conducts the test as a whole. The goal of system test is to test the functional or non-functional behaviors of the final product. It is tested against the system requirements. It also tests some behaviors that are beyond the system requirements.

3 .5 Maintenance Phase

After a product is released and put on the market. There still have some jobs to do, such as fixing the defects, updating the system when the rules have changed, the new requirement changes, or improving software for more efficiency. Any change in hardware or software shall require a new release, a new vision number, and perform the regression tests before the system is updated in the field.

When updating software remotely, the target shall check the origin of the source. Any code or data from the unauthorized source shall be rejected. And before the code transfer, all packets should be encrypted. Also, it is important to prevent the packets from being hijacked.

4 Evolution of Microprocessor/Microcontroller

Since the microprocessors were invented in 1970s, such as Motorola 6800 in 1974, the architecture of the microprocessors/microcontrollers have been improved a lot. Originated from Von Neumann Architecture (both instruction and data share the same memory) to Harvard Architecture (instruction and data don't share the same memory; they are stored in separate memories), the architecture of the microprocessors keeps evolving into the Modified Harvard Architecture.

The latest architecture of microcontrollers, such as ARM and PowerPC, is the Modified Harvard Architecture, i.e., instructions and data are stored in the same memory, but instruction and data are kept in the separated caches. From the same memory space, the CPU reads the instructions into the instruction cache, and reads data into the data cache. Then the CPU fetches instruction from the instruction cache for execution, and the CPU loads/stores data in the data cache.

Also, the instruction set was improved from Complex Instruction Set Computing (CISC) to Reduced Instruction Set Computing (RISC). Since RISC simplifies the instructions, it reduces a lot of transistors and circuitry, and improves the execution speed.

4 .1 Microprocessor vs Microcontroller

The difference between a microprocessor and a microcontroller is that micro-controller contains the peripherals, but the microprocessor does not.

4 .1.1 Microprocessor

A microprocessor contains the Central Processing Unit (CPU). It does not include the peripherals. It is designed to perform arithmetic and logic operations. The CPU fetches the instructions and decode the instruction. It also loads the data to the registers and performs the operations, and stores data from register to the memory. Typically, the CPU performs the operations that include adding, subtracting, and logically comparing two numbers. Some CPU may include the multiplication unit.

4.1.2 Microcontroller

A microcontroller includes Nested Vector Interrupt Controller (NVIC), caches, on-chip memory (RAM and flash), Floating-Point Unit (FPU), … etc. Sometimes it is referred to System-on-Chip (SoC). Since the microcontroller (MCU) has the on-chip peripherals, it can reduce the power consumption, the size, and the cost for the whole system.

There are many kinds of microcontrollers on the market. Usually, ARM Cortex-M processors are widely used in the small devices, while NXP PowerPC and Intel Pentium/Core processors are used in larger systems.

4 .2 Types of Processor Architecture

Since 1970s, the architecture of the processor CPU has changed dramatically. From a simple Von Neumann to Harvard architecture, then to Modified Harvard Architecture.

.2.1 Von Neumann Architecture

This type of the architecture consists of a control unit, Arithmetic and Logic Unit (ALU), memory and registers. The concept of Von Neumann Architecture is the instruction and data share the same memory space. The advantage of this architecture is simple, but the disadvantage is accessing both instruction and data at the same time is not allowed because there is only one shared memory. It slows down the memory access.

.2.2 Harvard Architecture

For Harvard Architecture, the instruction memory and the data memory are in separate units, and connected by two different buses. Both instruction and data memories can be accessed at the same time. So, fetching the instruction and accessing the data can be simultaneously. It speeds up the code execution, but the architecture is much more complicated.

4 .2.3 Modified Harvard Architecture

Another approach is keeping the instructions and data in the same memory, but provides separate instruction and data caches. This architecture is widely used in the modern processors. The instructions are read from memory into the instruction cache, and data is read from memory into the data cache, or written to the memory from the data cache.

Since the CPU can run much faster than reading instructions or data from the memory, to improve the efficiency of memory accessing, each memory access is a cache block size, i.e., multiple words. In this case, more instructions or data can be stored in the caches. It increases the cache hit rate (see section 4.4.2), and reduces the traffic of memory accessing.

4.3 CPU Core

A CPU performs fetching the instruction, decoding the instruction, executing the instruction, and loading/storing the data. When the CPU is powered, it starts to take actions. It brings up the whole processor. The CPU includes the following components:

4 .3.1 Arithmetic Logic Unit (ALU)

ALU is the most important building component of the CPU. It loads the data from the registers and perform the arithmetic or logic operations.

4.3.2 Sequencer

The sequencer decodes the instruction, and generates the address for the next fetching. If no branch is required in the code, it simply uses the address of the next instruction. If a branch is required, it generates the new address of the next instruction.

4 .3.3 General Purpose (Core) Registers

Generally, each CPU has 16 or 32 core registers which is a piece of memory temporarily storing the data for ALU operation. The size of the register is 32 bits for 32-bit CPU. The following is an example of ARM Cortext M7 sore registers. There are 16 registers in the register file. Only the low 13 registers are used for the general purpose. The high 3 registers are reserved for compiler: R13 is for stack pointer, R14 is for link return address, R15 is for program counter.

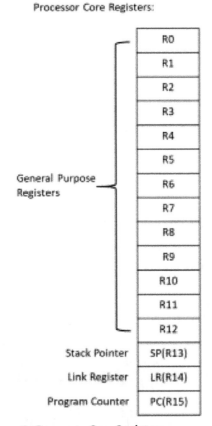

Figure 3: Processor Core Registers

4 .4 CPU Core Peripherals

In addition to the core, the modern microcontrollers are equipped more peripherals, such as NVIC, Cache, MMU, FPU, … etc. to ease the hardware design:

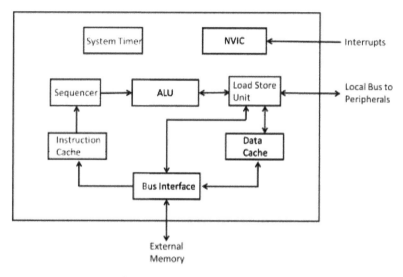

Figure 4 : CPU Core and Peripherals

4 .4.1 Nested Vectored Interrupt Controller (NVIC)

A Nested Vectored Interrupt Controller is a table where the CPU handles the exception and interrupts. The Interrupt Service Routine (ISR) or the address of the ISR is stored at the entry of the interrupt vector table. An exception is generated by the CPU when something related to the CPU goes wrong, such as the CPU tries to fetch outside the memory boundary. Unless there is some hardware support from the processor, usually it is hard to recover from an exception. An interrupt is generated by internal or external hardware, such as a timer has expired or an external event.

For ARM Cortext M4, the lowest position (offset 0) of the exception table is the end address of the stack (stack pointer). The next lowest position (offset 4) is the reset address where is the start of the code. After that, there are Non-Maskable Interrupt (offset 8), Hard Fault (offset 0xC), Memory Management (offset 0x10), Memory Access Fault (0x14), … etc. The higher priority interrupt (the smaller priority number) can preempt the lower priority interrupt (the larger priority number).

Here is an example of ARM Cortex M4 interrupt table. The lower the priority number has the higher priority.

Priority	Offset	Description
	0x0000	End stack pointer
	0x0004	Reset
	0x0008	NMI
	0x000C	Hard Fault
0	0x0010	Memory Management
1	0x0014	Memory Access Fault
2	0x0018	Undefined Instruction
	0x001C – 0x0028	Reserved
3	0x002C	System Service Call via SWI Instruction
4	0x0030	Debug Monitor
	0x0034	Reserved
	0x0038	PendSV
	0x003C	SysTick
	0x0040	IRQ0
	0x0044	IRQ1
	0x0048	IRQ2
	...	

Figure 5: ARM Cortex M4 Interrupt Vector Table

In many situations when an exception or interrupt occurs, there is no point for CPU to continue the execution. The ISR is just sitting in an infinite loop. The whole system is hung. If the embedded system has a Watchdog Timer (WDT) (see section 11), the processor can be reset by WDT (if WDT is configured), and start the code all over again from the beginning.

4 .4.2 Cache

The main memory for the CPU usually is not fast enough. CPU can execute the instructions in microseconds or nanoseconds. To get an instruction or data from the main memory takes much longer than the CPU execution time. If there is no cache support, when CPU is accessing the memory, it is blocked and waits for the completion of reading the instruction or the data from the main memory. The CPU time is wasted. So, cache plays a temporary memory for the instructions or the data.

Cache is a fast memory (SRAM). CPU works with the instruction cache and the data cache. If the instruction or the data is already in the cache, CPU can read it directly from cache without being blocked. Cache is not directly addressable by software. It transparently holds the recent instructions or data, and is solely controlled by the hardware. Software won't be able to program the cache.

Cache is divided into small fixed-size blocks. Each block (cache line) contains multiple words of instruction or data. Each block has an entry in the cache. When a block of memory is transferred from the memory to the cache, a cache entry is created. The entry includes the data, the starting address of the memory block, and the state of the cache line (see the next section).

4 .4.2.1 State of Cache Line

When the CPU tries to read or write a location in the main memory, it checks whether the address is in the cache or not. It may encounter one of the following situations:

- Cache hit – Data/instruction is in the local cache. The CPU simply fetches the instruction from the instruction cache, or reads/writes the data in the data cache. There no need to access the main memory.
- Cache miss – Instruction/data is not in the cache or the cache entry is invalid. CPU then fetches a block of instruction or data from the main memory into the cache. If the cache is full, the oldest or the least-accessed block is deleted to make the room for the new block. Then the new block of instruction or data is transferred into the cache.

- Cache dirty – The contents of the cache line have been modified. But the main memory is not updated.

4 .4.2.2 Cache Coherence

In a shared memory environment of multiple processors, each processor has its own data cache. In the cache of each processor may have a copy of the same data from the shared memory. One processor updates the data in its own cache, but not in the shared memory location. To synch with the data, other processors need to know the updated value. Cache coherence is designed to ensure that all processors have the same updated value in a timely fashion. Usually, cache coherence is only for the data cache, because there is no updated instruction in the instruction cache.

Here is an example of the cache coherence problem:

- Processor 1 (P1) reads data from memory location y. A copy of y content is transferred to P1's cache.
- Processor 2 (P2) also reads the same data from memory location y. A copy of y content is transferred to P2's cache.

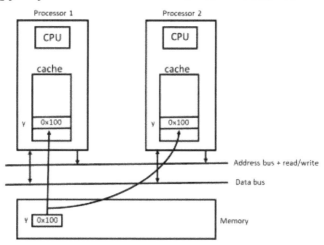

Figure 6: P1 and P2 Have Its Own Copy of y Value

- P1 increases y by 1 (y++). Since y is in P1's cache, so there's a cache hit. P1 updates its local cache without writing the updated data back to the memory location y.
- If P2 tries to read memory location y again (perhaps after synchronizing with P1), it will also see a cache hit. However, it will read an old value of y in its own cache. This can cause a problem.

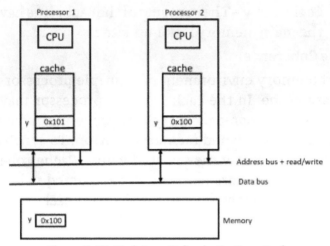

Figure 7: P1 Updates y Value in Its Own Cache

Some processors, such as NXP PowerQUICC II, use the Bus Snooping hardware to solve the cache coherence problem. This piece of hardware monitors the bus activity of the transactions which modify the locations of the cached data. The processor which modifies the data in the cache also needs to generate the invalidate signal to other processors. Here is how it works:

- When P1 updates memory location y, the cache generates an invalidate cache signal to other processors.
- When P2's snooping hardware sees the signal of the invalidate memory location y, and also finds a copy of memory location y in its own cache, it marks the state of the cache line of the memory location y as invalid.

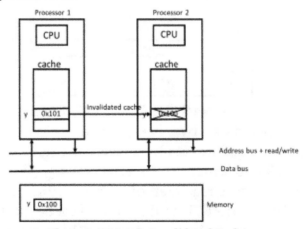

Figure 8: P1 Issues Invalidated Cache

- Now P2 tries to read memory location y again. It causes a cache miss, and initiates a data bus transaction of reading y from the main memory.
- When P1's snooping hardware sees the memory read for y, and detects the modified copy in its own cache, it emits a retry response that causes P2 to suspend the read transaction.
- Now P1 writes (flushes) the modified cache line back to the main memory.

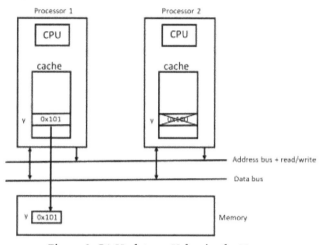

Figure 9: P1 Updates y Value in the Memory

- Then P2 can continue its suspended transaction and read the correct y value from the main memory.

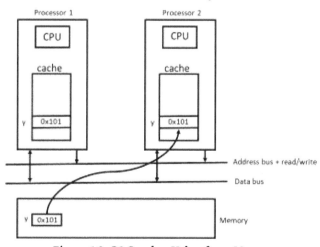

Figure 10: P2 Reads y Value from Memory

4 .4.3 Tightly Coupled Memory (TCM)

For some processor, such as ARM Cortex M7, TCM resides in the processor. It is a fast memory (SRAM) like cache. But unlike cache, software can control TCM. It can be configured as Instruction TCM (ITCM) and/or Data TCM (DTCM) by software. Software can store the code or the data in this memory. The CPU can fetch the instruction directly from ITCM or loads/stores data in DTCM. TCM is an expensive device in the processor. ITCM should hold only critical routines such as interrupt handling routines (ISR) or critical real-time tasks. DTCM should store critical data structures such as interrupt stacks.

Since TCM won't use the external bus, it reduces the power consumption and improve the performance.

4 .4.4 Floating Point Processing Unit (FPU)

An FPU coprocessor can perform the floating-point operations, such as addition, subtraction, multiplication, division, or square root. It has its own set of registers which are 32/64 bit-bit wide. IEEE 754 format is the standard format for most FPU. Without FPU, the compiler has to generate the floating-point simulation code for the floating operations. It is very slow. For some algorithm, FPU makes the algorithm possible for applications.

4 .4.5 Memory Management Unit (MMU)/Memory Protection Unit (MPU)

This unit provides the access privilege of memory pages, the change/reference status of each page, and the memory translation from the virtual address to the physical address. For many Real-Time Operating Systems (RTOS) that run the code in the virtual address space, MMU/MPU is a must (see section 14.3).

4 .4.6 System Interface Unit (SIU)

The SIU provides the interface mechanism to the processor. It consists the system configuration and protection, clock synthesizer, power management, and external bus interface. During the initialization, the developer needs to set up the registers in this section for those devices.

4 .4.7 Phase Locked Loop (PLL) and Clock Synthesizer

Most of the processor/DSP use the external clock source. Some processors have the clock crystal in the chip. In spite of the internal clock source, the processor allows the designers to bypass the internal clock and use the external clock. So, the designers can have the choice over the clock frequency they want.

When the external clock signal enters the processor, it goes through the Phase Locked Loop (PLL) which reduces the jittering and stabilizes the clock. Then the input clock is distributed to different clock sources, such as CPU clock, bus clock, baud rate generator, ... etc. Since those clocks have different speeds, the input clock can be multiplied to higher frequency or divided into slower frequency. Usually, the SIU registers provide the developer to choose the multiplication factor or the division factor for the frequencies.

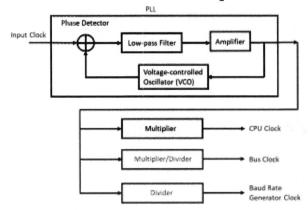

Figure 11: PLL and Clock Synthesizer

4 .4.8 System Timer

It also known as SysTick. Initially a count is loaded to the counter. The count is calculated from the frequency of the system clock or other clock source. When the count of the System Timer transitions from 1 to 0, it generates a SysTick interrupt. The count is automatically loaded to the counter after the time has expired. So, it generates periodic interrupts. It is used for the time keeping purposes or time measurement. Usually, the operating system uses the interrupts to handle the rescheduling of the tasks.

Here is an example of ARM Cortex-M System Timer. The count value in the Reload Value Register is only 24 bits. For the processor clock is 100 MHz, compute the count value for the 20 ms time interval (if the processor clock is selected as the clock source):

$$\text{Reload Value} = \frac{\text{Time Interval}}{\text{Clock Period}} - 1$$

$$= \frac{20 \text{ ms}}{10 \text{ ns}} - 1$$

$$= ((20 \times 10^{-3}) / (10 \times 10^{-9})) - 1$$

or

$$= (20 \times 10^{-3} \times 100 \times 10^{6}) - 1$$

$$= 2000000 - 1$$

$$= 1999999$$

$$= 0x1E847F$$

Figure 12 : System Timer Count Computation

4 .4.9 General-purpose Timers

The developer can configure the General-purpose Timers for keeping time. When the timer expires, it can generate an interrupt. So, the software can utilize the interrupt to perform the tasks. Sometimes, the timers are only 16 bits, but they are allowed to concatenate 2 timers together to become a 32-bit timer. For the processor that does not have the System Timer, the developer can use the General-purpose Timer to generate the system ticks.

The General-purpose Timer also can be programmed to generate and output a periodic waveform.

4 .4.10 Direct Memory Access (DMA)

A DMA controller can move data to or from the memory without the intervention of the CPU. Software can set up the DMA descriptor(s) and registers, then it initiates the DMA controller to start transferring. The CPU can continue doing other operations while the DMA is transferring.

The DMA controller requests the bus access. When the CPU is not using the data bus, the CPU grants the bus to the DMA controller. So, the DMA can use the bus to transfer the data. To check if the transfer is done or not, software can either poll the DMA status register to check the transfer completion or the DMA controller can generate an interrupt to the CPU when the transfer is done.

The DMA controller not only can do "memory-to-memory", it also can transfer data from peripherals, such as UART data buffers, to the memory or vice versa.

4 .4.11 Parallel IO Ports

For each processor, there are many IO pins for communicating to the outside of the processor. Those pins are bi-directional, and grouped into ports. Each port may have 16/32 pins. And there are corresponding registers (16/32 bit) for each port. Developers can program the port registers to configure each individual pin.

Usually, the pin functions are multiplexing. Software is able to program the port registers to configure each pin for the pin function. Depending on the function, each pin can be:

4 .4.11.1 General Purpose IO (GPIO) Pins

The direction of each pin can be programmed by software as the input pin or the output pin in the register.

- If a pin is set for input, reading the data register will receive the state of that pin.
- If a pin is set for output, writing to the data register will output the state of the pin. Be careful, not all pins in the same port are for output or all output pins change their state. In order to change the state of one pin, read that data register to obtain whole port pins, and modify only that pin, then write the whole port pins back to the data register. Another concern is: during reading, modifying, and writing sequence, the state of some pins may get changed. Although the chance is slim, it might happen. Some ARM processor provides Bit-banding feature to solve the read-modify-write problem. But the feature is beyond the scope of this book. It is up to the reader to discover.

4 .4.11.2 Interrupt Pins

Some of the input pins can be used as interrupts for the external events. Like other interrupts/exceptions, the interrupt service routine (ISR) is stored in entry of the NVIC. Those pins can be programmed as edge interrupt or level interrupt. The difference between edge interrupt and level interrupt is explained in section 10.

4 .4.11.3 Dedicated Function Pins

Some pins can be configured as dedicated function pins for communicating with the peripheral devices, sch as I^{2}C, UART, SPI, Ethernet, USB, ...etc. It is very difficult or impossible to provide each individual pin for all the peripheral devices. To reduce the pin outs, those function pins may be multiplexing, i.e., a specific pin can be configured as one of the function pins, but not more than one function. Depending on the applications, not all the peripheral devices will be implemented in a product. The designers can choose the devices they need, and configure port pins for the devices. The process of manual selection of the function pins can be complicated. The good news is that many processor/DSP manufacturers provide the tool for designer to choose the function pins without causing the conflicts.

For example, if Port A pin 11 can be multiplexing, it can be configured as either I^{2}C Serial Data pin (see section 6.2) or SPI MOSI signal (see section 6.1). But it cannot be configured for both functions at the same time. If a product needs SPI interface, this pin can be configured as the SPI MOSI pin, but not the I^{2}C Serial Data pin.

After choosing the dedicated function pins, each selected device has configuration registers. Those registers need be programmed by software. The reference manual and the datasheet provide the good information about how to configure those registers.

5 Digital Signal Processor (DSP)

Similar to microprocessor/microcontroller, DSP also has improved dramatically since 1980s. Texas Instrument (TI) TMS320 family debuted in early 1980s. The Harvard architecture DSP was only 16-bit fixed point processor, and ran 5 MHz clock at that time. It included a MAC (multiply-accumulator), cache, and memories. The recent multiple processing units DSP, such as TMS320C67xx, makes a big difference in processing power.

Back in 1980s, in order to perform the image processing, it needed a special designed array processor to do the job. For example, the edge enhancement for a CT image was done by the array processor. The collected data was in the space domain, and was stored in a 2-dimentional array. The array processor converted the data in each row of the array into the frequency domain by using the Fast Fourier Transform (FFT) algorithm. Then in the frequency domain, a high pass filter was applied to the frequency data. Finally, the frequency data was converted back to the space domain for display. This required a lot of processing power, especially the FFT. Nowadays a DSP can do the same job much faster than the array processor.

5 .1 Types of DSP Architecture

In order to improve the throughput, DSP evolves from simple processor into complicate multiple processing units. Now it can reach thousands of MIPS or MFLOP. It also speeds up the peripherals which communicate to the external devices. Here are some different types of DSP architecture:

5 .1.1 Multiply-Accumulate (MAC)

The MAC architecture can speed up the operations of multiplying-then-adding with the previous sum. This type of DSP benefits the computation of signal filtering, such as FIR, IIR. When multiplying two arrays of data, and adding the previous result, MAC can do the both operations in the same instruction.

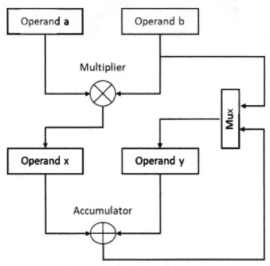

Figure 13: MAC Architecture

Texas Instrument TMS320C54x DSP has a 17x17-bit multiplier coupled with a 40-bit adder for nonpipelined single MAC instruction.

5 .1.2 Superscalar

Superscalar uses hardware to accomplish the parallel computing. The CPU fetches multiple instructions and tries to figure if those multiple instructions can be processed in the same cycle. It has deep pipeline. Since it uses hardware to check the dependency, it increases the hardware complexity, the cost, and decreases the flexibility. Now superscalar architecture is not so popular.

5 .1.3 Multiple-Processors

Another approach to accomplish the parallel computing is Very Long Instruction Word (VLIW). In mid 1990s, Texas Instrument introduced the new DSP architecture. For example, TMS320C62xx has two banks of processors. Each bank has 3 adders, and a multiplier. So, there are total 8 processing units. Each processing unit has 32 bits instruction code. So, the instruction word can be up to 256 (8 x 32) bits long. But when not all 8 units are used in a clock cycle, the code of the unused processor will be excluded from the instruction word which then becomes shorter (less than 256 bits).

Each bank has 16 32-bit general-purpose registers (In some C67x DSP, the register file is increased to 32 32-bit registers). Each processor can read directly from and write directly to the register file within its own bank. However, there is cross path which allows the processor from one bank to accesses a 32-bit operand in the register file on the other bank.

VLIW utilizes the compiler to figure out the instruction parallelism in advance. During the compile time, the compiler checks the instructions and figures out the possibility of arranging as many operations as possible in the same clock cycle. The processors just execute the instruction.

Not only the compiler takes care of the processing unit's parallelism, it also takes care of the pipeline operation of instructions, i.e., the operation may have the delay slot(s). For example, in TMS320C674x DSP, a 16 x 16 multiplication has one delay slot. The operation takes 2 cycles to complete. The product of the multiplication won't be available in the destination register in the next cycle. It will be in the register a cycle later. However, during the delay slot, the result from the previous multiplication instruction can be available.

Generally, the DSP compiler can do a good job to create efficient instructions. If a cycle does not utilize all 8 processors, the compiler then generates a shorter instruction (less than 256 bits). But the developer also can help the compiler by arranging the code for compiling. When a loop of computing an array of data, the inner loop is most time consuming. If the code can make the inner loop to the minimum instructions, it can save a lot of computing time.

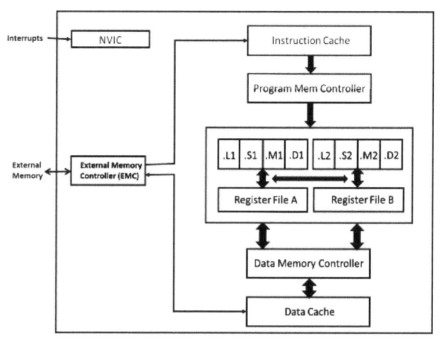

Figure 14: TI TMS320C6xxx DSP CPU and Core Peripherals

5 .2 DSP Core Peripherals

Similar to microcontroller, DSP has NVIC, Instruction and Data Caches, Memory Protection Unit, General-Purpose Timers, DMA, Host Port, ... etc.

6 Processor/DSP Peripherals and Communications

In the real world, the processor needs to get data from the external devices, such as the temperature sensor, the accelerator, the gyro, ...etc. The processor/DSP provides the wired inter-chip communication to those devices. Usually, it is the serial communication. But why not use parallel communication? Does the parallel interface provide a faster communication? The reason is the reliability. To make all parallel lines to work together is difficult at high speed. So, the serial communication is more reliable.

The serial communication needs only few lines: the data line(s) and a clock. It has less lines than the parallel communication. For transmitting, data is put on the data line at either the rising edge or the falling edge of the clock. The receiver gets the data on the rising edge or the falling edge of the clock. The transmitter and the receiver have to sample on the same edge. The following example illustrates how the data are transmitted or received on the serial lines. The same input data for both the raising edge and falling edge sampling, but the output data are different.

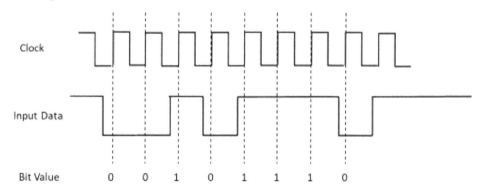

Figure 15: Sample on Clock Raising Edge

If sampling on the raising edge of the clock (see above figure), the output data bits are "00101110".

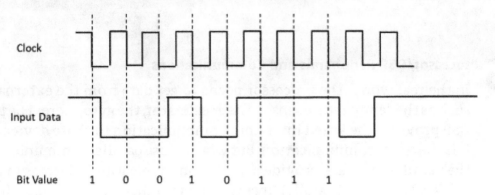

Figure 16: Sample on Clock Falling Edge

If sampling on the falling edge of the clock (see above figure), the output data bits are "10010111"

6 .1 Serial Peripheral Interface (SPI)

SPI is a simple 4 wired master-slave communication. Those wires are:

- SCLK: Serial Clock (output from the master)
- MOSI: Master Output, Slave Input (output from the master)
- MISO: Master Input, Slave Output (output from the slave)
- $\overline{SS}$: Slave Select (active low, output from the master)

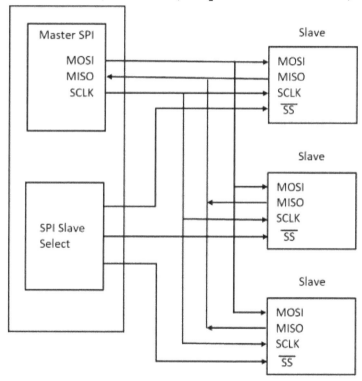

Figure 17: SPI Single-Master and Multi-Slave Configuration

SPI is meant for short-distance communication. There is a transmit line, and a receive line. So, it is asynchronous, and full-duplex. A master can control more than one SPI device. When the master is ready to send data, it brings the slave device select signal ($\overline{SS}$) to low (active low signal), generates the clock (SCLK), and puts the command on MOSI line. For some device, it requires the SCLK signal stays high when not using. So, the clock duty cycle starts transitioning to low. When the receiver (slave) gets the command, it puts the requested data on MISO line. The master then receives the data from the slave. In the following example, the master puts the command, 0x2E (00101110)_b on the MOSI line. When the slave receives the command, it puts the data on the MISO line, So, the master gets the data, 0x4C (01001100)_b.

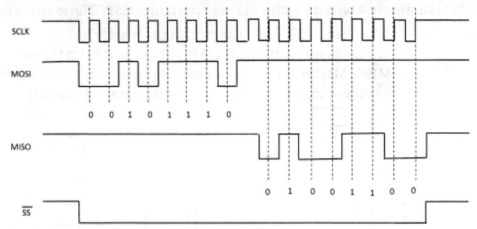

Figure 18: SPI clock and data buses

Usually, the microcontroller has the dedicated interface for the SPI. But the slave select line is not in the dedicated interface. It is defined by one of the GPIO pin. If there is no SPI interface on the microcontroller or the product needs more SPI devices on the system than the SPI interfaces provided by the microcontroller, in either case, designers can use 4 GPIO pins for those 4 SPI communication lines. One of the 4 pins is dedicated to the serial clock. Software code can toggle the line to generate the clock duty cycle.

6 .2 Inter-Integrated Circuit (I2C/I2C)

I^{2}C has even less signals between the master and the devices. The master can communicate to more than one I^{2}C devices. Unlike the SPI that uses the different slave select line ($\overline{SS}$) to choose the device, I^{2}C uses the address to communicate to the slave device. Each slave has its own address which is only 7 bits for most of the devices. I^{2}C needs only two signals:

- SDA – Serial Data
- SCL – Serial Clock

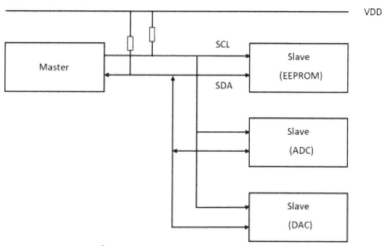

Figure 19: I^{2}C Single-Master and Multi-Slave Configuration

For reading, the master generates the clock, sends a read request to the slave device on SDA line, and waits for the ACK and the result from the slave. When the slave receives the request, it sends back the ACK first, then sends the result back to the master on SDA line. Depending on the size (how many bits) of the result, the master needs to keep the clock (SCL) running until all bits reach the master on SDA line. If the read result is 16-bit long, the clock needs keep going for another 16 duty cycles after sending the request. So, the master can receive the result. If the clock is cut off right away after the master sends the request, the read result won't be able to reach at the master, even though the slave puts the result on SDA line.

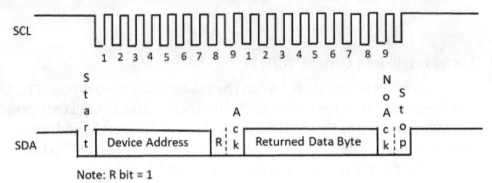

Note: R bit = 1

Figure 20: I²C Master Read Timing

For writing, the master generated the clock, sends a write request to the slave, and waits for the ACK from slave. After the master gets the ACK, it sends the write data to the slave, and waits for the ACK.

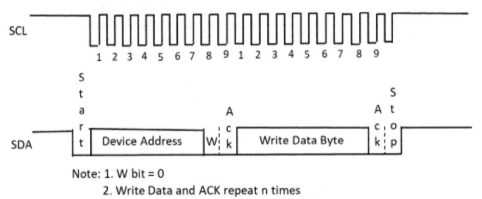

Note: 1. W bit = 0
      2. Write Data and ACK repeat n times

Figure 21: I2C Master Write Timing

6 .3 Universal Asynchronized Receiver and Transmitter (UART)

UART is commonly used for debugging purpose in the embedded system. Unlike the UNIX system or PC, an embedded system does not have the monitor to show the progress of the code. It relies on the target to send ASCII messages to the COM port on the host (such as PC) for debugging. So, the developer can know what's going on at the target. It also allows the developer to send ASCII messages to the target.

UART uses two basic signals, transmit and receive. The sender puts the data on the transmit line which is connected to the receive line of the receiver. There is no clock associate with the data transmitting. UART requires both transmit side and receive side to set up the same baurate. When the receive line transition from high to low (start bit), the receive side uses an internal clock that runs 8x, 16x, or 32x faster than the baurate, and samples each bit of the incoming data at least 2 times faster in the center of the bit. The transmitter and receiver have the same baurate and protocol. After receiving the fixed number of bits, the receiver gets the stop bit, and then stops the clock. Since there are separate lines for transmit and receive, it is asynchronized communication, and full-duplex.

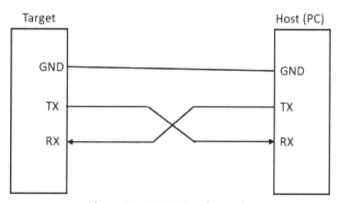

Figure 22: UART Configuration

For each character is sent, there are 10 (no parity) bits or 11 (with parity) bits are transmitted. If the baurate is 115200, each bit width is 1/115200 second. The order of the bits is:

    1. Start bit

2. Data bits (8 bits)
3. Parity (optional)
4. Stop bit

The following figure is an example that an ASCII character "M" is transmitted. The parity bit is optional. If the parity bit is transmitted, it could be 0 or 1 depending on the even parity (to make the 1-bit count to even count) or odd parity (to make the 1-bit count to odd count). In this case, the parity is set to even parity. There are 4 1-bits. So, the parity bit is set to 0.

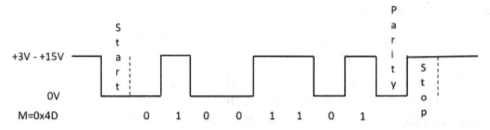

Figure 23: UART Data Transmitting

Nowadays, the 9-pin connector is not supported by the PC makers. Instead, the USB port replaces the 9-pin connector on the PC. An USB-to-UART converter is used for the communication between the target and the host (PC).

The most used function in C language is "printf". On the PC or the Linux System, it is easy to use "printf" function to output a message on the console. The C code links with the libraries during the build. And when the caller is ready to send a message, it just passes the format string, and parameters to "printf" function. The character string will show up on the console.

But in the embedded system, it is a little bit complicated. Without the OS support, developers have to create their own "printf" function or get it from the libraries. This function takes a format string, and variable number of parameters. It basically performs the following operations. Here is only a very simple example. It could get much more complicated when the format involves in floating point conversion. For example, printf("the format string", parameter1, parameter2, ...);

- Call va_start() to set up the pointer to the first parameter.
- It runs in a loop to parse through each character in the format string.
- If the character is not '%' sign, save the character in the output

buffer.
- If the character is '%' sign, read the next character.
- If the next character is 'c', call va_arg() to get the character and put the character in the output buffer.
- If the next character is 'd', call va_arg() to get the integer and call itoa() to convert the integer into a string of decimal. Save the string in the output buffer.
- If the next character is 'x', call va_arg() to get the integer and call itoa() to convert the integer into a string of hexadecimal. Save the string in the output buffer.
- If the next character is 's', call va_arg() to get the pointer of the string and copy the string to the output buffer.
- At the end of the parsing, call va_end().
- Finally, call the UART driver to send out the output buffer.

Another usage of UART is the interface to Global Navigation Satellite System (GNSS). The GNSS sends the data to other system, or other system sends a command to the GNSS.

6 .4 Universal Serial Bus (USB)

The USB device in the embedded system is used for dumping data to On-the-Go (OTG) flash drive or communicating to the host. When the embedded system collects data and stores the data in the RAM or in the flash, those data can be dumped to the flash drive. The data can be used for off-line analysis on the PC.

For some processors that provide Serial Wire Debug (SWD) can use the USB port to communicate with the debug tools on the host (PC).

6 .5 Ethernet

Ethernet is another fast serial communication. It is the Link Layer that is commonly used in the Local Area Network (LAN). For the embedded system, it provides the following functions:

- For a multi-board embedded system, the communication between boards can be established by Ethernet. Data can be passed between the boards.
- Ethernet also can transfer data to other embedded systems or receive data from other embedded systems.
- For debugging purpose on an embedded system, through the Ethernet connection, the target can communicate with the debug tools on the host (PC).

Each Ethernet node has its own MAC (Media Access Control) address (6 bytes). All the nodes on the network are listening to the frames all the time. When a node needs to send a frame, it waits for the network to become silent for a period of time (frame gap), then sends the frame. The receiver checks the frame. If the destination MAC address in the frame matches the receiver's own MAC address or the destination address is the broadcast address (0xFFFFFFFF), the receiver accepts the frame, else it discards the frame.

6 .5.1 Ethernet Frame

When the system is ready to send a message, it divides the message into frames if the message is longer than 1500 bytes. The structure of a frame includes:

- Destination Address – The 6-byte MAC address of the receiver or the broadcast address (0xFFFFFFFFFFFF).
- Source Address – The 6-byte MAC address of the sender.
- Type/Length – This 2-byte field can be used as the payload length or the Ethernet Type. When the value in this field is under 1500, it indicates the length of the payload. If the value is over 1536, it indicates the Ethernet Type.
- Payload Data – This field contains the message data for transport. The length of the payload is from 46 bytes to 1500 bytes. If the data is shorter than 46 bytes, pad the payload. So, the length is at least 46 byes.
- Frame Check Sequence (FCS) – It is the calculated 4-byte CRC (Cyclic Redundancy Check, see section 6.8) value of the above 4 items, but not FCS self. The sender side computes the CRC and appends the CRC after the Payload field. After receiving the frame, the receiver side performs the CRC checking. If there is no CRC error, the frame is accepted.

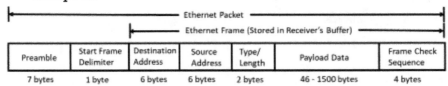

Figure 24: Ethernet Frame/Packet Structure

6 .5.2 Ethernet Packet

At the physical layer, the frame is assembled with Preamble and Start Frame Delimiter (see the above figure) to construct an Ethernet packet. The Preamble is a 7-byte sequence of alternating 1's and 0's (10101010, 10101010, ..., 10101011). It provides the known pattern to other nodes to synchronize the receive clock. The Start Frame Delimiter signals the beginning of the frame. After a packet is transported, there is an interpacket gap which usually runs about 96 bits.

6 .6 High-level Data Link Control (HDLC)

HDLC is the synchronous data link layer (layer 2) protocol which is defined by ISO (International Organization for Standardization). It relies on the physical layer for clocking and synchronization for transmitting and receiving.

HDLC uses bit-stuffing scheme (zero insertion/deletion) to ensure that information data never matches the opening/closing flag (01111110), i.e., when the information data has consecutive five 1-bits, a 0-bit is inserted. When the receiver sees five 1-bits, it drops the next 0-bit. So, the data is recovered.

The transmission data is structured in frames. Multiple buffers can be sent in a frame. When a frame is ready for transmit, the controller gets the Opening Flag (0x7E=01111110), address, control, information, then starts sending the frame. When the last buffer in the frame is sent, a 16/32-bit CRC and a Closing Flag (0x7E=01111110) are appended at the end.

Opening flag	Address	Control	Information	CRC	Closing flag
8 bits	8 bits or more	8 or 16 bits	Variable length, 8xn bits	16 or 32 bits	8 bits

Figure 25: HDLC Framing Structure

When the receiver is activated, it waits for the Opening Flag (0x7E) of the frame. After receiving the Opening Flag, it then gets the address and compares the address with the previously defined address. If the address match is detected, the receiver controller starts transferring the incoming frame into the empty buffers. If the address is all ones, this frame is for broadcasting. Also, the controller gets the incoming frame.

While receiving the data, the controller checks the frame length to avoid the received data overrunning the buffers. At the end of the frame, the controller checks the received CRC with the recalculated CRC. If the CRC is correct, the CRC and the frame length are appended at the end of the last buffer.

6 .7 Analog-to-Digital Converter (ADC) and Digital-to-Analog Converter (DAC)

The real world is analog. But analog signals are hard to manipulate. In order to process the input data, the analog signal is converted into the digital data by ADC. The digital data is processed by the digital processor or DSP, such as filtering or enhancement. Then the processed digital data is converted back to the analog signals by DAC.

Take the sound for example. To eliminate the noise from the sound, the sound goes though the ADC. The continuous wave of sound is sampled, then quantized to the discrete digital data. The noise can be filtered out through the digital processing. The filtered digital data is converted back to the analog wave. So, human can hear the clear sound. Although filtering the noise can be done by the analog filter, but it is not as precise and flexible as the digital filter which is part of the code and can be adjusted easily.

According to the Nyquist-Shannon Sampling Theorem, the sample rate has to be at least 2 twice of the frequency. So, if the frequency is 100 Hz, the sampling rate must be at least 200 times per second.

6 .8 Cyclic Redundancy Check (CRC)

Since CRC is widely used in the networking communication and in the tele-communication, it is worth to understand how it works. It is an error-detecting scheme. The algorithm is based on the polynomial division. A bit stream is divided by the CRC divisor. The remainder of the division becomes the CRC. The bit length of CRC divisor may vary depending on the communication protocol. 32-bit CRC is the most commonly used in the network communication, such as Ethernet, and HDLC. The CRC polynomial divisor for 32-bit CRC is:

$$G(X) = X^{32} + X^{26} + X^{23} + X^{22} + X^{16} + X^{12} + X^{11} + X^{10} + X^8 + X^7 + X^5 + X^4 + X^2 + X + 1$$

The bit pattern of the above polynomial coefficients is 33 bits because in order to obtain a 32 bits remainder, the divisor has to be 33 bits. Since the highest order (X^{32}) of the polynomial coefficient is always 1, it is dropped. The following bit stream is for the serial communication that the most-significant bit (msb) is transmitted first:

31 28	27 24	23 20	19 16	15 12	11 8	7 4	3 0	(bit)
0000	0100	1100	0001	0001	1101	1011	0111	(coefficient)
0x0	0x4	0xC	0x1	0x1	0xD	0xB	0x7	= 0x04C11DB7

For many serial communication protocols, least-significant bit (lsb) is transmitted first, such as Ethernet, and HDLC. For the lsb transmission first, the order of the above bit stream is reversed (bit 0 to bit 31). Here the bit pattern of the lsb first is:

0 3	4 7	8 11	12 15	16 19	20 23	24 27	28 31	(bit)
1110	1101	1011	1000	1000	0011	0010	0000	(coefficient)
0xE	0xD	0xB	0x8	0x8	0x3	0x2	0x0	= 0xEDB88320

There are two approaches to calculate the CRC-32 of a byte array (lsb first transmission):

6 .8.1 Compute CRC32 On-The-Fly

For each byte in the array, it starts to calculate from the least-significant bit and loop through all 8 bits. After finishing all bytes in the array, the polarity of the CRC32 bits is flipped, i.e., 0's becomes 1's, and 1's becomes 0's. Here is the sample code:

```
// Compute CRC32 On-The-Fly
crc32 = 0xffffffff;
for (lenIndx = 0; lenIndx < messageLength; ++lenIndx)
{
  byte = message[lenIndx];
  crc32 = crc32 ^ byte;
  for (bitIndx = 0; bitIndx < 8; ++bitIndx)
  {
    if (crc32 & 0x01)
    {
      crc32 = (crc32 >> 1) ^ 0xEDB88320;
    }
    else
    {
      crc32 = crc32 >> 1;
    }
  }
}
crc32 = ~crc32;
```

Figure 26: Compute CRC32 On-The-Fly

6 **.8.2 Table-driven**

First, build a CRC32 table of 256 words. Here is the sample code to build the CRC32 table:

```
void buildCRC32Table(uint32_t crcTable[256])
{
  uint32_t tabIndx, bitIndx;
  uint32_t crc32 = 0;

  for (tabIndx = 0; tabIndx < 256; ++tabIndx)
  {
    crc32 = tabIndx;
    for (bitIndx = 0; bitIndx < 8; ++bitIndx)
    {
      if (crc32 & 0x01)
      {
        crc32 = (crc32 >> 1) ^ 0xEDB88320;
      }
      else
      {
        crc32 = crc32 >> 1;
      }
    }
    crcTable[tabIndx] = crc32;
  }
}
```

Figure 27: Build CRC32 Table

Then loop through each byte in the array. Use the byte value to generate the index to the table. Fetch the word from the table. Then compute the CRC32. At the end, the polarity of the CRC32 bits is also flipped. Here is how to use the CRC32 table:

```
// Table-driven CRC32
tabCrc32 = 0xffffffff;
for (lenIndx = 0; lenIndx < messageLength; ++lenIndx)
{
   byte = message[lenIndx];
   tabIndx = (byte ^ tabCrc32) & 0xFF;
   tabCrc32 = (tabCrc32 >> 8) ^ crc32Table[tabIndx];
}
tabCrc32 = ~tabCrc32;
```

Figure 28: Compute CRC32 through Look-up Table

The table-driven approach has less computations. It is commonly used in the software implementation.

7 How to Choose a Microcontroller or a DSP

Traditionally the designer of an embedded system focused on hardware only or hardware first. But as the system gets more and more complicated, a lot of aspects need be considered when choosing the hardware. Most of the time, software is trailing behind the hardware, and the complexity of software is getting worse. Without good software tools, it is very difficult to develop and debug the software. Nowadays software plays an important role in selecting a microcontroller or DSP.

Usually, the microcontroller/DSP manufacturer provides the reference manual, the programming manual, datasheets, and the processor architecture reference manual. They are good source about the detail information for choosing the processor/DSP. Those manuals are also very helpful during the design and implementation for hardware and software. Another good source is the Field Application Engineer (FAE). The chip manufacturers or the distributors have FAEs to help their customers to choose a processor. They even help the customers to solve problems if the customer uses their products.

Here are some of the considerations for choosing a microcontroller or DSP:

7 .1 Throughput (Benchmark)

In a computing intensive system, it is important to figure out the MIPS (Million Instructions Per Second) or MFLOPS (Mega Floating-point Operations Per Second) of the whole system. A processor or a DSP must have enough processing power to accomplish the job. Without enough processing power, the microcontroller or DSP is not applicable to the system. It won't meet the timing requirements.

For each algorithm in the system, figure out how many operations of additions, subtractions, multiplication, division, and shifting, ... etc. Add the counts together. Make sure the microcontroller or DSP can handle all operations in a timely manner.

Also, it is a good practice to reserve some processing power for the future improvement. The system might need to add some new features. If there is spare processing power, it is easier to make the changes in the software than changing the hardware.

7 **.2 Cost of the Material**

Unless for some strategic reasons, almost all the commercial products are built for profits. Cost is very sensitive to a product. If the cost is too high, the manufacturer may need to lose money to sell the product. Without affecting the quality, always take the cost into consideration when choosing a processor, a DSP or other hardware components. This is even more true for the consumer products. A small increase in the cost will eat up the profit.

Other cost cutting is using software to replace the hardware functions. In this way, it not only reduces the number of parts, also shrink the PCB size. The BOM (Bill of Materials) cost can be lowered.

7.3 Life Span

How long will the processor/component continue? After a processor/component has been on the market for a long time, the supplier may end the production of the processor/component for variable reasons. Make sure the processor or any components will last as long as the product life cycle. For some avionic products, they will remain on the market for more than 20 years. So, it is important to consider the life span of the processor/component.

For the regulatory industries, it is hard to get the product approved by the government. If the supplier decides to stop the production of the processor/components after the product is approved, one way to secure the manufacturing of the product is to buy enough quantities of the processor/components. Through the monthly production, estimate the amount of the processor/components that are needed in the future, and purchase those parts in advance.

7 .4 Peripherals

If a processor/DSP already has the build-in interface to the peripherals, such as SPI, I2C, UART, Ethernet, USB, etc., it can save money and reduce the design time. When adding the external peripherals interface to a processor/DSP, it not only increases more risks, but also needs more hardware tests in the future. If the processor/DSP supports the build-in hardware interface to the peripherals, it is much easier for the hardware design and test.

The same reason applies to the External Memory Interface (EMIF). Many processors or DSP's support seamless interface to the external memory, such as SRAM, DRAM, and flash. If the memory interface is already supported, hardware engineers can focus on the design, instead of looking into the memory interface.

7.5 Power Consumption

Power consumption is very important for the embedded systems, especially for wireless devices, portable devices, and IoT products. For example, the user always wishes that the handset battery can last longer. So, the battery does not need to be frequently charged. Or the IoT devices are installed in the remote area where the regular electricity cannot reach. Replacing batteries is very difficult. In this case, battery life is crucial. So, power consumption needs to be taken into consideration when choosing a processor and other components.

7 .6 Hardware and Software Tool Support

Hardware design tools include the EDA (Electronic Design Automation) software, emulator, and HDL (Hardware Design Language) simulator. Those are important tools for hardware engineers during hardware designing.

Some processors have the parallel IO pins that are multiplexing for peripherals, such as SPI, I2C, UART, ... etc. If the processor company provides the tool for selecting the peripheral pins without conflicts, engineers can just enter the peripherals that they need, then the tool will select which pins in the IO ports for the peripherals. They don't need to spend time on how to select those pins by hand.

What kinds of software does this processor/DSP come with? It is important to have software tools, such as compiler, assembler, linker, debugger, real-time OS, simulator, and software libraries. If the processor/DSP maker provides Integrate Development Environment (IDE) tools, those tools help the developer to implement and debug the code with less efforts. If the chip maker doesn't provide the IDE tools, check whether there are third-party IDE tools that are available for the processor/DSP.

Another consideration is the Real-time OS (RTOS) support. Due to the assembly language involved in the RTOS, not all the processors have the RTOS support. Also, check if the RTOS needs an MMU or MPU in the processor for virtual to physical address translation. It is necessary to check with the RTOS company to clarify it.

7 .7 Security Support

Securing the data and firmware become an important subject in the modern embedded systems, especially for IoT products. Not only the code and firmware need be secured, it also important to protect the data during transmitting. If the transmitted data must be encrypted, it may require the hardware to accelerate the encryption/decryption process. Or there is a requirement that needs the true random-number generation. The hardware random-number generator can accomplish the job quickly.

If the system involves in RSA Public-Key encryption and decryption (see section 21), in addition to the random number generator, hardware also needs to check whether the generated random number is a prime number or not, to find the encryption/decryption keys, to raise the message exponentially, and to do the modulo operation. These operations require a lot of computations. Hardware support is essential to accomplish the encryption/decryption job in real time.

Some ARM processors add the Platform Security Architecture (PSA) and Trust-Zone which protect the data, allow software to run the secure environment and non-secured environment, perform the authentication check, and use secure Inter-Process Communication (IPC) API library to exchange data. This kind of technology helps the designers to meet the security requirements.

7.8 Choose the Right Frequency

If there are processor/DSP and RF devices on the same circuit board, it is important to look into the frequency of the processor/DSP. When the processor/DSP is running, the clock frequency or accessing the hard drive may affect the RF frequency. The processor frequency generates the harmonics which can interfere with the RF frequency.

To bear in mind that the faster clock rate of a processor/DSP consumes more power, and generates more heat. Power consumption and the ventilation of heat need be taken care of.

8 Big-Endian vs Little-Endian

Big-endian and little-endian are the terms that describe the order in which a sequence of bytes is stored in the memory.

8 .1 Big-Endian

Big-endian is an order in which the "big end" (most significant value in the sequence) is stored first (at the lowest storage address). For example, in a big-endian processor, the four bytes (or an unsigned integer) for the hexadecimal number 0x6789ABCD would be stored as 6789ABCD in memory (i.e., 0x67 is stored at memory address 1000, 0x89 will be at address 1001, 0xAB will be at address 1002, and 0xCD will be at address 1003).

For most of the RISC microprocessors, such as PowerPC and ARM, and Motorola microprocessors use big-endian. The most significant bit in a 32-bit register of the big-endian processor is bit 0. The least significant bit of the register is bit 31. Here is the example from NXP MPC8280 microcontroller:

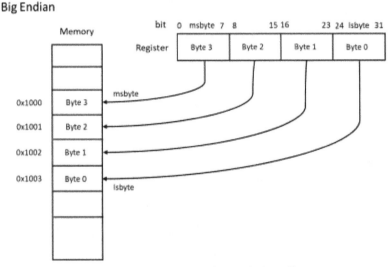

Figure 29: Memory vs Register of Big Indian

Big-endian (Note: Byte 0 is LSByte)

Byte 3 at addr 0	Byte 2 at addr 1	Byte 1 at addr 2	Byte 0 at addr 3	Word at addr 0

Halfword 1 at addr 0 | Halfword 0 at addr 2

Byte 3 at addr 4	Byte 2 at addr 5	Byte 1 at addr 6	Byte 0 at addr 7	Word at addr 4

Halfword 1 at addr 4 | Halfword 0 at addr 6

Byte 3 at addr 8	Byte 2 at addr 9	Byte 1 at addr 10	Byte 0 at addr 11	Word at addr 8

Halfword 1 at addr 8 | Halfword 0 at addr 10

Byte 3 at addr 12	Byte 2 at addr 13	Byte 1 at addr 14	Byte 0 at addr 15	Word at addr 12

Halfword 1 at addr 12 | Halfword 0 at addr 14

Figure 30: Word Storage of Big-Indian

8 .2 Little-Endian

Little-endian is an order in which the "little end" (least significant value in the sequence) is stored first. In a little-endian system, an unsigned integer (32 bits), 0x6789ABCD, would be stored as CDAB8967 in the memory (i.e., 0xCD at address 1000, 0xAB at 1001, 0x89 at 1002, and 0x67 at 1003).

Intel and AMD processors use the little endian. The most significant bit of a 32-bit register of the little-endian processor is bit 31. The least significant bit of the register is bit 0. Here is an example of Intel Core i7 processor:

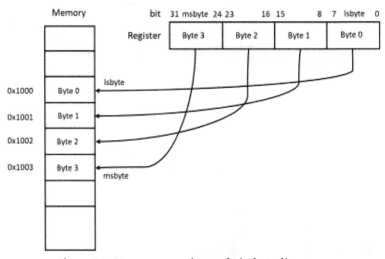

Figure 31: Memory vs register of Little-Indian

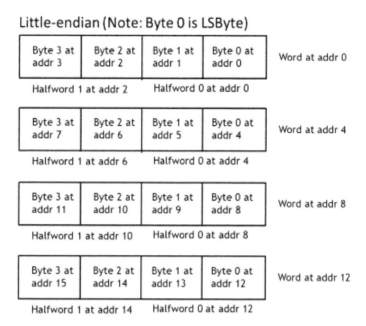

Figure 32: Word Storage of Little-Indian

9 Memory

Memory is a storage which holds the data and instructions that are used by the CPU. For the embedded system, memory size is limited. Developers have to write efficient code that meets the requirements. Also, designers have to decide where the code will be executed, from the flash or RAM? It takes longer to fetch the code from the flash memory. But if the code is executed from RAM, the code need be copied from the flash to RAM in the bootloader, and requires a larger size of RAM. Here are several types of memory:

9 .1 Volatile Memory

Volatile memory works only when the power is applied. It loses the contents when the power is lost. There are two most commonly used RAM: Dynamic Random-Access Memory (DRAM) and Static Random-Access Memory (SRAM).

9 .1.1 Dynamic Random-Access Memory (DRAM)

Currently DRAM is the most widely used memory. It has the high capacity which can reach 16G (1G x 16) bits in a single chip. It is used for storing the data, and the code to be executed. Although DRAM is slower than SRAM, it is cheaper than SRAM.

DRAM must be periodically refreshed. Usually, the microprocessor or micro-controller provides the memory configuration registers to configure the refresh rate of DRAM. Many processors have provided seamless interface to external DRAM, but the refresh rate for each DRAM may be different. So, the developer has to configure the refresh rate.

9 .1.2 Static Random-Access Memory (SRAM)

SRAM does not need to refresh constantly. So, it has higher speed than DRAM. But it is more expensive, and the capacity is not as large as DRAM. It is typically used for CPU cache.

9 .2 Non-Volatile Memory

Unlike RAM, the content of the Non-Volatile Memory stays in the memory after power is off. When the power is restored, the content is the same as before.

9 .2.1 Flash Memory

Flash memory is used for preserving the code and the data. It is divided into blocks (sectors). So, each block can be erased and programmed independently. There are two types of flash memory: NAND and NOR.

- NAND memory – The cells are divided into sectors (blocks). Write, read or erase operations are based on the sector. If a byte in the NAND flash memory needs be updated, the whole sector is read into RAM, update that byte in RAM, erase that sector in flash, and write the whole sector from RAM to NAND flash memory. It has higher density than NOR. Therefore, NAND is mostly used for storage, such as thumb drives, SD cards, … etc.
- NOR memory – It allows a single word, half word, or byte to be written to an erased location. But it takes longer and more power to erase and write the NOR flash memory. It also allows to read a single word, half word, or byte. It is used in the application that needs random access.

When the CPU fetches the instruction or data from the flash memory, it needs more wait states to read because the flash memory is slower than RAM. But the flash memory is widely used to store the code and data. When the processor boots up, the CPU first reads the flash memory to start executing the code.

For the RAM, software can write to the RAM directly. But for the flash memory, there are certain commands to erase, or program. Usually, those commands are detailed in the flash memory datasheet. Some third-party vendors provide the flash chip programmer, such as Lauterbach TRACE32, but developers can write their own code to program the flash memory.

Here is the algorithm to program a value to one address at a time for the 16-bit NOR flash memory (Micron M29FxxxFT/B). This command requires 4 write operations. The final write operation latches the address and the data. The following address offset is the offset from the flash memory address.

1. Write 0xAA to address offset 0x555.
2. Write 0x55 to address offset 0x2AA.
3. Write 0xA0 to address offset 0x555.
4. Write the data to the desired address.

This command only writes a 16-bit word to the flash. Some other commands allow the code to erase a whole block (sector) of the flash, enter the "UNLOCK BYPASS" mode, then use "UNLOCK BYPASS PROGRAM" command to program the whole block. At the end, exits the "UNLOCK BYPASS" mode. This is much faster to program the flash because "UNLOCK BYPASS PROGRAM" command needs only 2 write operations.

9 .2.2 Electrically Erasable Programmable Read Only Memory (EEPROM)

Similar to flash memory, EEPROM uses electric field to erase and write. But EEPROM requires an electronic device or a special voltage to program it. It is not used for storage any more. Nowadays, it is used for smart cards or remote keyless systems.

9 .3 Dual Port Memory

Dual-ported RAM (DPRAM) is another type of random-access memory that allows multiple reads or writes to occur at the same time, or nearly the same time. Unlike single-ported RAM which only allows one access at a time, DPRAM allows 2 processors to access the same memory.

Video RAM or VRAM is a common form of dual-ported dynamic RAM. It is mostly used for video memory which allows the CPU to draw the image, and at the same time the video hardware is reading the image out to the screen.

9 .4 Error-Correcting Code (ECC) Memory

In the aerospace, avionics, and financial industries, memory error is not acceptable. A single bit flip can make a huge difference in the result. For example, an integer stored in the memory is zero. When the CPU reads the integer from the memory, a bit of the integer is flipped to 1. The CPU gets a non-zero integer. The code checks whether the integer is zero or not in an "if" statement. But the read integer is not zero. In this case, the result is totally different. Therefore, any memory failure could cause disasters.

As DRAM is running faster and faster, and the density is getting higher and higher, DRAM is becoming vulnerable to electrical, radiation, and magnetic interferences. To ensure the processor reads the correct data from memory, ECC can detect and correct a single bit error in a 64-bit data transfer, and detect a double-bit error. An ECC double-bit error will generates an exception to the CPU.

Modern chip makers and memory makers work together to implement ECC scheme to protect the data integrity. Some ARM Cortex-M processors and PowerPC PPC-8280 have the memory controller that supports ECC.

10 Interrupt

An interrupt is an event generated by hardware. It can be an event from the internal or external of the processor. Then the event informs the CPU that something has happened, and needs the CPU to take action.

10 .1 Types of Interrupt

The interrupt can be an edge interrupt or a level interrupt.

- Edge Interrupt – The interrupt gets fired when the interrupt line transitions from high to low or from low to high of a pulse. Usually, the transition of the interrupt line is from high to low. After the pulse, the interrupt line returns to the original level.

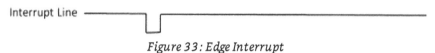

Figure 33: Edge Interrupt

- Level Interrupt – The level interrupt gets fired when the interrupt line transitions from high to low and stays low or from low to high and stays high until the ISR clears the interrupt. Then the interrupt line returns to the original level.

Figure 34: Level Interrupt

10 .2 Interrupt Service Routine (ISR)

Each entry of the interrupt vector table, such as ARM Cortex-M processors, is 4 bytes. It stores only the starting address of the ISR. But for some processors, such as TI TSMC6746 DSP or PowerPC PPC8280, each entry of the interrupt vector is 256 bytes. So, a small ISR (less than 256 bytes) can be stored in the interrupt vector. If the ISR is larger than 256 bytes, the ISR can branch to other address outside the interrupt vector.

In response to the interrupt, the CPU suspends the currently running routine or program, fetches the starting address of the Interrupt Service Routine (ISR) from the entry of the Nested Interrupt Vector Controller table (NVIC, see section 4.4.1), then starts executing the ISR. When the ISR is done, the CPU restores the suspended routine or program. Just like a subroutine call, at the beginning of the ISR, the contents of the registers and the return address are stored. When the ISR finishes, those contents are restored, and the CPU branches to the return address.

Depend on the design, the interrupt table can reside in the RAM or in the flash. The table is created during the code build. And it is mapped to the beginning of the flash memory. So, the CPU can fetch the boot code when it is powered on. The bootstrap can move the table from the flash memory to the RAM if necessary. If the interrupt table resides in the flash memory or ROM, the addresses of the ISR have to be placed in the entries of the table during the linking time.

Under the RTOS environment, the interrupt table is moved to the RAM. The RTOS provides the API routine for the application software to install the ISR to the interrupt table. The application is not allowed to access the interrupt table directly. If there is no operating system, the application can write the starting address of the ISR to the entry of the interrupt table.

Note: Never wait for an event or resource in the ISR. It will cause the CPU to halt, and waste CPU time. Moreover, the event may never come, or the resource may not be ready. The whole system will be locked.

10 .3 Priorities of Interrupt

When the CPU is serving an interrupt, and another higher priority interrupt occurs before the current ISR finishes, the current ISR is suspended and the higher priority ISR starts to run. After the higher priority ISR finishes, the current ISR is resumed if there is no more higher priority interrupt is pending.

Here is an example of the nested interrupts. The lower IRQn number has the higher priority. So, IRQ1 has the highest priority, and IRQ3 has the lowest priority.

- When there is no interrupt, all interrupt lines are quiet.

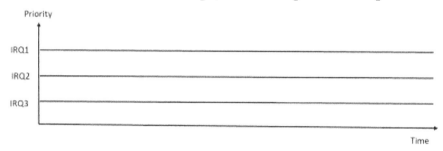

Figure 35: No Interrupt

- Then IRQ2 interrupt occurs. The IRQ2 ISR starts to execute because there is no higher priority interrupt.

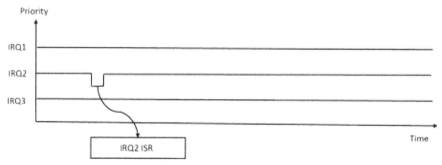

Figure 36: IRQ2 Interrupt

- While IRQ2 ISR is running, IRQ3 interrupt occurs. Since IRQ3 has the lower priority, IRQ2 ISR keeps running, and IRQ3 interrupt is pending.

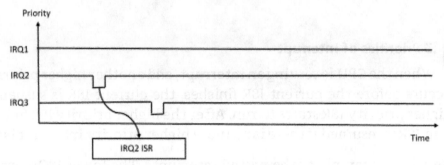

Figure 37: IRQ2 Interrupt and IRQ3 Interrupt

- Then the higher priority interrupt, IRQ1 occurs. IRQ2 ISR is suspended. IRQ1 ISR starts to execute.

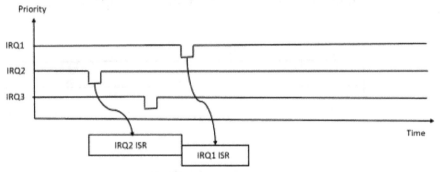

Figure 38: IRQ2 Interrupt, IRQ3 Interrupt and IRQ1 interrupt

- When IRQ1 ISR finishes, IRQ2 ISR is resumed.

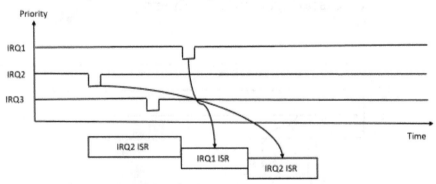

Figure 39: IRQ2 Interrupt and IRQ3 interrupt

- After IRQ2 ISR finishes, the lower priority interrupt, IRQ3 ISR, starts to execute.

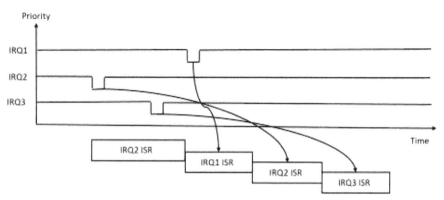

Figure 40: IRQ3 Interrupt

11 Watchdog Timer (WDT)

In an embedded system, when something goes wrong due to either software or hardware failure, such as software is stuck in an infinite loop, the system is hung. A watchdog timer is used to rescue. It can reset the processor without human intervention.

When the system is powered on, WDT is not activated. WDT starts when it gets the first pet from software. After the WDT starts, software has to keep petting the WDT within a certain period of time, such as every 200ms. If the watchdog timer is not petted in 200ms, WDT will reset the processor. So, the CPU can start again from the beginning. Usually, the reset line of a processor is active low. WDT holds the reset line low for some time, and releases it. Then the processor comes out of the reset, and starts the code execution from the beginning.

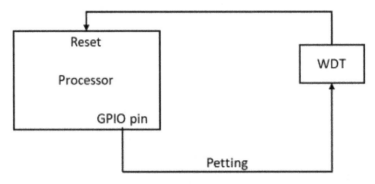

Figure 41: Watchdog Timer Configuration

The petting of WDT should use the application software. Do not use the timer interrupt ISR to pet WDT because when the software crashes, the interrupt might be still working. Petting may keep going. The processor will never get reset. Petting can be achieved by toggling a GPIO pin at certain period of time by the application software. So, when the system crashes or other code is stuck in an infinite loop, the petting code cannot pet WDT anymore. WDT will reset the CPU, and the system starts from the beginning.

12 Hardware Prototype

To get some confidence before the massive production, hardware engineers can build a breadboard if the board is small and not complicated. For a large system, usually only several prototype boards are built for checking. Hardware engineers can check the power, capacitors, resistors, memory (address and data lines of RAM and flash), and trace the signals. During the manufacturing, if the pull-down or pull-up resistor is missing, it could change the state of the signal. Check if "Do Not Stuff" (DNS) is open. Or some wires might be crossed over each other, and cause a short circuit.

Software developers can provide the hardware bring-up code to help hardware engineers to debug. The bring-up code has intensive memory test, drivers for the I/O tests, ... etc. Later, the bring-up code can evolve into the production code. After the prototype boards are checked and fixed, those boards can be distributed to other teams to start their tasks. They are not wasted. They can be used by the hardware test team, software team, system team, and V&V team. Those teams can start developing the code or the test plan.

13 Software Components

Software could get complicated. Without proper design and development, it could get out of control. The code could tangle together. It ends up very difficult to debug and fix the bugs, or for the future expansion. It need be carefully designed, and divided into small components, and set up the communications between the components.

13.1 Software Layers

From the top to the bottom, software can have several layers. On the top is the application layer, and flows down to hardware at the bottom. Each layer has its own functions, and can be further divided into components.

Bootloader

Application Code
Application Programming Interface (API)

RTOS	Middleware

Hardware Abstraction Layer (HAL)
Board Support Package (BSP) and Drivers
Hardware

Figure 42 : Software Layers

- Application – The application code implements the functional requirements. It processes data that is received, such as the user input, or the data that is generated by the lower layers and passed to the user.
- Application Programming Interface (API) – The API code is designed for the application code to call the RTOS or the middleware without the knowledge of how it works. For example, the middleware library provides the API routines. The application code just calls the routines to retrieve or deliver the data.
- Real-Time Operating System (RTOS)/Middleware – RTOS can ease the headache of the interaction between tasks (see section 14.2). Middleware is the agent between different systems/platforms. It provides the service to the application. It includes the stacks, such as TCP/IP stacks, USB stack … etc.
- Hardware Abstraction Layer (HAL) – HAL is a set of routines that provide the interface to the hardware. It provides the routines that interact with the hardware subsystems. Without knowing how hardware works, developers just call those routines to communi-

cate with the hardware.
- Board Support Package (BSP) and Driver – BSP contains a package of drivers and configurations that access the specific hardware. To support different processors or platforms, BSP and the driver use the compile options to pick up the processor or the platform. The compiler can pick up the piece of the code according to the option. For example, ARM Cortex-M4 and M7 may have different drivers. Therefore, they have different compile options.
- Boot Code – The first code to be executed when the power of the processor is turned on (see section 17).

13.2 Security

As mentioned in the requirement, "security through isolation", the software components can be easily categorized into secured components and non-secured components. The secured components can be hidden in the secured environments. Since software is broken into small pieces, the hacker needs to spend more time to break the whole system.

13 .3 Component Testing

While designing the software, bear in mind that software testability is very important. Each component has a specific function, and is independently developed. If there is a change in the code, the change should be confined in the related components, and it is easier for the developer to test those components again.

14 Bare Metal System vs Real-Time Operating System (RTOS)

Depending on the software requirements, the designer has to evaluate whether a RTOS is needed or not. It depends on how complicated the software is. To help software to meet the requirements, RTOS provides some features, such as Task Management, Scheduling, Inter-Task Communications, Interrupt Handler, Memory Management, or maybe the File System.

14 .1 Bare Metal System

A bare metal system has an executive which runs in an infinite loop. The executive checks the events in the polling style. If there is an event, the executive process the event. After it finishes the event, it checks the next event. The events are processed sequentially.

This method is alright for non-timing critical system. The critical event has to wait until its turn. There is no priority among the events. It is easy to implement at beginning. But as the system grows larger and larger, it becomes difficult to add more functions, and difficult to maintain.

Here is an example of the bare metal system. An embedded keyboard has a microcontroller that is running in an infinite loop. It utilizes the periodic timer to control the timing. Every time the timer has expired, the timer ISR increase the interrupt count by one. Since human's typing is much slower comparing to the processor, it is not necessary to check the activities in each loop. Instead, the executive checks the count in the loop. If the count has reached at the desired number, it checks the activity of the keyboard. If a key is hit, it figures out which key. After taking care of the debounce, finally it confirms the key typing.

In the same loop, the executive can also check other devices, such as the mouse, the track ball, touch panel, … etc. at different time intervals. Each device is checked at its own interrupt count.

14 .2 Real-Time Operating System (RTOS)

A Real-Time OS is the operating system that takes action immediately when the data comes in or an event occurs, and assigns a task to take care the data or respond to the event. It is able to serve the time critical event. Usually there is only very short delay to take the action. Depending on how critical the system needs to react, there are two types of real-time requirements:

- Hard Real-Time – An event need be taken care by hardware or software within the constrained time. If hardware or software cannot complete the function within the defined time, the system is considered as fail.
- Soft Real-Time – The event can be completed beyond the confined time. It won't cause the system to fail.

A typical RTOS provides the following services. Some RTOS requires Memory Management Unit (MMU) or Memory Protection Unit (MPU) for virtual addressing.

14 .2.1 Task Management

In the RTOS environment, software code is broken up into tasks. A task is a functional unit. It requires thoughtful design to create a task. If there are too many tasks, the communication between them is difficult. Nonetheless, too-less-tasks makes the task too complicated to handle. Also, how to assign the priority to each task needs well arranged. Task management must prevent the deadlock from happening.

A task usually has the following features:

- A priority is assigned to the task.
- The task has its own stack.
- Allocate the local variables in the stack.
- Perform the task initialization.
- It runs in an infinite loop.
- At the beginning of the loop, it waits for an event.
- If there is no event, it is blocked by RTOS.
- After receiving the event, it is resumed, and starts to execute the application functions.
- When finishing the application functions, it returns to the beginning of the loop.

For each task, when it is spawned, it gets the initialization done first, then enters an infinite loop. First thing in the loop is checking for the event, such as mutex, semaphore, or mailbox. If there is no event, it enters the blocked state. When the event occurs, it is woken up by RTOS and starts to execute the code if there is no other higher priority task is running. When it reaches the end of the loop, it loops back to the beginning of the loop to check for the next event.

Most operating systems appear to allow multiple tasks to execute at the same time. This is called multi-tasking. In reality, each processor core can only be running a single thread of execution at any given point in time. Depending on the priority of the tasks, the multi-tasking system is able to suspend a task, and resume the task.

14.2.2 Scheduling

In typical designs, a task has three states:

- Running – Executing on the CPU.
- Ready – Ready to be executed.
- Blocked – Waiting for an event, I/O for example.

The scheduler is responsible for deciding which task to run. The developer can choose one of the following algorithms for scheduling:

14.2.2.1 Round Robin

It is a preempted scheduling. Each task is assigned with a fixed time slice (quantum time). All tasks are listed in a request queue and executed in a circular order. The queue is first come first served (FCFS). They all have the same priority. If a task needs more than the quantum time, it is preempted and appended at the end of the request queue. The blocked task has to wait until all other tasks in front of it have been served. Then it can be executed again. If a task finishes before the time out, it quits and the next task on the queue can start to run.

14.2.2.2 Priority

Each task is assigned with a priority (from 0 to 255). Usually, the lower priority number has the higher priority. For the preemptive scheduling, the higher priority task preempts the lower priority task whenever the higher priority task is ready to run. It is similar to the interrupts (see section 10). For the non-preemptive scheduling, the higher priority task has to wait for the current task to finish, then it starts to run.

14.2.2.3 Preemptive Fixed Priority and Time-Partitioning

In the avionics system, some critical applications must have a certain amount of processing time in each time-partitioning. Some RTOS products, such as Deos™ from DDC-I Company, have met this requirement. Deos™ has the following features:

- The scheduling uses the system tick as the time-partitioning.
- Each task is assigned with a fixed priority and a time budget.
- Each task is also assigned to the time-partitioning. For the critical tasks, they are scheduled in every time-partitioning. Other tasks can be scheduled every other time-partitioning or every 3 time-

partitioning, ... etc.

- Within a time-partitioning, tasks are scheduled according to the priority. The higher priority task gets executed first. If a task finishes before the time budget, it releases the CPU time to other tasks. If a task cannot finish within the time budget, it is suspended. Later it can be resumed to use the "slack" time in the same time-partitioning or in other time-partitioning when there is no higher priority task is running.

- This RTOS also provides the space partitioning which restricts a task from modifying another task's memory without authorization. In this way, the lower priority task does not interfere with the higher priority task.

Here the "slack" time is the remainder of the time in a time-partitioning after all scheduled tasks have finished until the next time-partitioning (see the following figure).

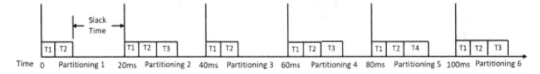

Figure 43: Combination of Priority and Time Slice Scheduling

In this example, the system tick is 20ms which is generated by the System Timer (SysTick see section 4.4.8). At the beginning of each time partitioning, the scheduler looks for the scheduled tasks. In Time Partitioning 1, only T1 and T2 tasks are scheduled. Since T1 has higher priority, T1 is executed first. When T1 finishes or time-out, T2 is executed. In this partitioning, there is no other task is scheduled to run after T1 and T2 complete their tasks. If a suspended task needs to use the slack time, it can continue to run after T1 and T2. Otherwise, the CPU runs the idle task, and waits for the next time partitioning. Time Partitioning 3 has the same situation as Time Partitioning 1.

In Partitioning 2, T3 is executed after T1 and T2 has finished their jobs. If T3 cannot finishes in Time Partitioning 2, it can continue after T1 and T2 in Time Partitioning 3 because there is only T1 and T2 are scheduled in Time Partitioning 3. Time Partitioning 4 and 6 have same situation as Time Partitioning 2.

In Time Partitioning 5, T4 is executed after T1 and T2 finish. After T4 finishes, if there is no task that needs the slack time in this partitioning, the CPU runs the idle task.

14 .2.3 Inter-task Communications

There are three most commonly used schemes for the inter-task communication in RTOS:

- Mutex – Mutex means Mutual Exclusion. When multiple tasks share a resource, only one task can access the resource at a time. So, the task that is accessing the resource can lock the resource. Other task that tries to access the resource has to wait for the resource to be unlocked. In some cases, this might cause deadlock.

- Semaphores – Unlike mutex, semaphores are signaling. When many tasks share a resource, the resource can be locked if it is used by one of the tasks. Another task wants to use the locked resource has to wait until the resource is unlocked. For example, in the producer-consumer case, there are 3 buffers between them. The maximum semaphore count is 3. The initial count is 0. The producer wants to write data to one of the buffers, it checks the count. If the count is less than 3, it locks the semaphore for writing to one of the empty buffers. When the writing is done, the producer increases the count by one, and unlocks the semaphore. The consumer has to wait for the semaphore to be unlocked. When the semaphore is not being locked, the consumer checks the count. If the count is greater than 0, it reads one of the buffers, and decreases the count by one.

- Mailbox – For Mutex and Semaphore, there is no data passing directly between the tasks. They rely on the predefined buffers for passing messages. But through the Mailbox, one task can send a message to another task. The message can contain a lot of data, and they can be queued. Tasks are able to communicate with one another to coordinate the activities or to share the data. In general, mailboxes are much like queues. Multiple messages can queue up. Most of the time, the queued messages are read in the first come first serve basis. But in some RTOS, the developer can prioritize the mailbox messages. A higher-priority message will be read before lower-priority messages, regardless of the order in which they are put in the mailboxes.

14 .2.4 Interrupt Handlers

When RTOS is in place, all the interrupts are handled by RTOS. Developers can install the ISR through RTOS API calls. When the ISR has finished and returns, the scheduler can take over and schedule the next task to run.

14 .2.5 Memory Management

Some RTOS provides the dynamic memory allocation which is convenient. But in embedded system, memory leak or insufficient memory can kill the whole system. Also, there is memory fragmentation problem, and it is possible that the system runs out of memory. The static memory allocation is preferred in the embedded system. At the beginning of the application, all required buffers are created for the future use.

Under RTOS, there are two kinds of heap: system heap, and task stack. Those big buffers can be allocated in the system heap which can be seen to other tasks. Each task has its own stack. All local variables, and buffers are allocated in the stack. How big stack is needed for a task? The developers have to figure it out. If the stack is too big, it is waste of memory. But if the stack is too small, it could cause stack overflow which is very difficult to detect. Some newer processors use hardware to detect the stack overflow.

14 .2.6 File System

Usually, file system is not needed in an embedded system. Only few RTOS's provide the file system. A file system can ease the pain of storing different kinds of data. Data can be stored with a filename in the file system. Those data can be retrieved later with the filenames.

14 .3 Physical Address vs Virtual Address

When there is no operating system involved (Bare Metal System), the code is running in the physical addressing mode. Many operating systems are running in the virtual addressing mode. In this case, the processor needs to provide the MMU/MPU which can translate the virtual address into the physical address.

14 .3.1 Physical Address

Physical address is the memory address that the CPU uses to access the memory. Before the CPU can access the instruction or the data, those instructions and data have to be stored in the memory spaces. Through the physical address, the CPU can fetch the instructions, and read/write data from/to the memory. Although for a 32-bit address bus, the physical memory space could reach up to 2^{32} (4 G) bytes, in reality the memory size in an embedded system is pretty limited. So, the physical memory space is much smaller than 4 G bytes.

14 .3.2 Virtual Address

Virtual address is the address used by the CPU during execution. It is managed by MMU/MPU, and the operating system which creates a page table. With the help of MMU/MPU, the CPU can obtain the physical address from the virtual address. Regardless the size of the physical memory space, for a 32-bit address bus, the virtual memory space can be as big as 2^{32} (4 G) bytes. When the operating system spawns a process, it allocates a chunk virtual memory for the code and the data storage, and maps the executable code/data into the virtual memory space. So, each process has its own virtual memory space. The virtual memory spaces of the processes are not overlapped each other because the virtual address can range from 0 to $2^{32} - 1$. It provides the protection for each process.

14 .3.2.1 Page Table (PT)

A page table is created by the operating system, and stored in the RAM. It contains the mapping information between the virtual address and the physical address. The table is a data structure that provides the flexibility of implementation, and enhances the performance of the address translation through the Translation Lookaside Buffer (TLB) in the MMU. Depending on the page/block size, the page table has many entries. Each entry (PTE) contains the address descriptor. The MMU uses the address descriptor to generate the physical address, the protection information, and the access privilege. The operating system has to program the registers in MMU/MPU to pass the starting address and the size of the table to the TLB.

When the page table gets too large to store the entire table in the RAM, portion of the table entries can be moved to the secondary storage, such as the flash memory or the disk. For example, for a 32-bit system, the virtual memory space is 4 G Bytes (2^{32}). If the page size is 4 Kbyte (2^{12}), there will be 1 M (2^{20}) entries when the whole virtual memory space is used. Each entry requires 4 bytes to hold the address descriptor. It needs 4 Mbyte of RAM to maintain the page table. It takes too much space in the RAM in an embedded system. So, some PTEs are stored in the secondary storage.

14 .3.2.2 Translation Lookaside Buffer (TBL)

The TLB is a piece of hardware that resides in the MMU. Usually there are 2

TLBs: one of the TLBs is for data translation (DTLB), and the other is for instruction translation (ITLB). The virtual address translation can be turned on or off. When the translation is turned off (such as Bare Metal System), the TBL uses the "virtual address" as the "physical address". There is no address translation.

By default, the TBL is turned off. When the TLB is turned on through the register in the MMU, the TLB acts like the cache for the page table. It stores the recently-used page table entries (PTEs). When a translation of virtual address is needed, the MMU looks for the entry in TLB first. If the entry is found in the TLB and the access is allowed, the MMU generates the physical address.

If an entry is not found in TLB, the MMU starts walking through in the page table in RAM to search for the PTE. If the entry is found in the page table and the access is allowed, the PTE is written back to the TLB. So, the address translation continues.

If the entry is not found in the page table either, the MMU generates a page fault. The operating system needs to take actions. There are two possible reasons to cause the page fault:

- As mentioned above, if the page table is too large, some PTEs are stored in the secondary storage. If the PTE is found in the secondary storage, and the access is allowed, the operating system then brings the PTE to the page table in the RAM, and updates the TLB. So, the address translation continues.
- The virtual address is invalid. This is caused by a process trying to access the memory space that doesn't belong to the process, such as the stack overflow or programming error.

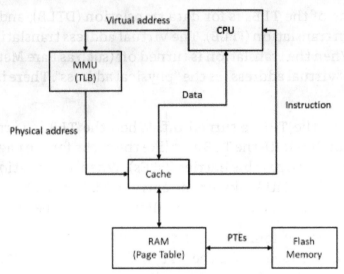

Figure 44: Virtual Address Mapping

14 .3.2.3 The Benefits of Virtual Addressing

The benefits of the virtual addressing are:

- Each process has its own address space. When a process tries to access the memory location outside its own virtual memory space, it will cause a memory fault exception.
- The virtual memory space is larger than the physical memory space. For example, an embedded system has only 8M Bytes of physical memory. The physical memory address is from 0 to 0x7FFFFF $(2^{23} - 1)$. But the virtual address can range from 0 to $2^{32} - 1$ (4 G bytes). So, the virtual memory space for each process is not overlapping.
- The virtual addressing also has the security benefit. It is hard for the hacker to load a process under the virtual addressing environment.

14 .4 Is RTOS Required?

The benefits of having RTOS are:

- Software components – Breaking up the application code into smaller components, such as tasks.
- Multi-tasking and concurrent processing – More than one task can run at the same time. Without RTOS, tasks are running sequentially. When one task finishes, then the next task starts to run. In RTOS environment, to let the higher priority task to run, a running task can be suspended before it finishes. Later the suspended task can resume the execution.
- Easier for future expansion – Under RTOS, a task is a complete unit. A new task can be easily added in the future.
- Predictable timing – Tasks are scheduled by the OS. It is easier to predict when the task will run.
- Robust task switching – According to the task's priority, the tasks are switched in and out. The developers don't need to arrange which task to run.
- File system – Some RTOS provides the file system. For some embedded system that needs to use the file system, RTOS can save a lot of time and energy.

The drawbacks of RTOS are:

- Increase memory size – RTOS will take some memory space, although it is not a huge code. Usually, the RTOS kernel is pretty small.
- Use CPU time – RTOS needs time to handle interrupts, scheduling, communication, and some management work.
- Longer learning curve at beginning – Engineers need more time to learn how to use it.

Whether an embedded system product needs a RTOS or not depends on the complexity of the software and hardware. Before choosing a RTOS, the designers need to evaluate whether RTOS is needed, and to check whether the RTOS supports the processor. Depending on the CPU and the complexity of the software, the designers can make the decision. Here are some thoughts:

- High-end CPU with complicated software – RTOS can be beneficial or even essential. An RTOS can help software to be better organized.
- Low-end CPU with complicated software – A simple RTOS kernel can ease the software design or provide a good platform for the future expansion.
- High-end CPU with simple software – RTOS may not be necessary. But the use of RTOS can help for the future software expansion.
- Low-end CPU with simple software – In this case, there is no need or benefits of RTOS unless the future software expansion will become more complicated.

15 Integrated Development Environment (IDE)

IDE provides tools, such as the text editor, the project creator, loading code to the target, debugging tools, the assembly window, the register window, the memory window, … etc. Under IDE, software developers can create a project, create files, write code, compile and link the code, download the code to the target, and debug the code. IDE has the Graphical User Interface (GUI) that creates a user-friendly environment. After setting up the IDE, the developer can easily (relatively) use it. Some IDE even provides the GPIO pin assignment or the PLL clocks selecting for the hardware design.

Eclipse is a free open source. Many large chip makers develop their own IDE based on Eclipse framework. The IDE is in cooperate with GNU C/C++ toolchain and GDB for ARM processors, NXP PowerPC processors, or TI's Code Composer Studio. The chip makers usually give away the IDE tools for free, but the user has to use their processors to get the benefits from the free tools.

15 .1 GNU Toolchain

A toolchain is a collection of software tools, such as compiler, assembler, linker, libraries, ... etc. GNU toolchain includes makefile, compiler, C library, assembler, linker, and debugger (GDB). GNU compiler is a cross-compiler which can generate the target executable code from a host, such as PC. The compiler supports a variety of processors, such as ARM processors, and NXP PowerPC processors. GNU toolchain is widely used in the embedded system field.

15 .1.1 Makefile

In a non-GUI environment, developers use Makefile to build the executable image. Not only for the final release version, but also for developing the code. It convenient to type "make" on the command line to build the whole image, but the developer needs to manually create the makefile. A Makefile includes the following functions and rules:

- List of files to be built, including C files, C++ files, assembly files, … etc.
- Setting rules for compiling, and assembling options, including the compile optimization level.
- Setting rules for linking, including the linker script, the libraries, the order of object files.
- It can include other makefile.
- At the end, it cleans up the unneeded files, such as the compile intermediate files.

Makefile can get very complicated. It is beyond the scope of this book to discuss in details. Here is a simple example of GNU makefile:

```
# Makefile
CC        := powerpc-motorola-elf-gcc
LD        := powerpc-motorola-elf-ld

TARGET  := mainapp
PROGRAM := $(TARGET).exe
LIBS   :=

# GNU Compiler
#   -O3     Optimize strongly
#   -g      Include debugging information
#   -c      Generate obj file
CCFLAGS  := -O3 –g -c

# GNU Linker
#   --script  Specify proper load location
#   -Map      Create map file
LDFLAGS  := --script=$(TARGET).ld -Map $(TARGET).map

OBJ       := maincore.o system.o uartdrv.o adspDrv.o
INC       := defs.h command.h

$(OBJ): %.c $(INC)
   $(CC)   $@ $< $(CCFLAGS)

$(PROGRAM): $(OBJ)
   $(LD)   $(OBJ) $(LIBS) $(LDFLAGS)

clean:
   rm -f $(OBJ)
```

Figure 45 : Sample of GNU Makefile

15 .1.2 Linker Script File

The main purpose of the script file is to describe the MEMORY definitions, and the SECTIONS definitions of how the input sections to be mapped to the link output file, and the order of the input sections. From the figure below, the linker script may look like:

```
// File name: mainapp.ld

MEMORY {
   // 32MB of dram starting at 0x00000000
   dram_memory : ORIGIN = 0x00000000,   LENGTH = 32M

   // 8M of flash starting at 0xfff00000
   flash_memory : ORIGIN = 0xfff00000,      LENGTH = 8M
}

CONSTANTS {
  heap_reserve = 1M
  stack_reserve = 512K
}

SECTIONS {
//
// RAM SECTIONS
//
   .sdabase      ALIGN(8) : > dram_memory
   .sdata                 : > .
   .sbss                  : > .
   .data                  : > .
   .bss                   : > .
   .heap         ALIGN(16) PAD(heap_reserve)  : > .
   .stack        ALIGN(16) PAD(stack_reserve) : > .

//
// ROM SECTIONS
//
   .text                  : > flash_memory
   .syscall               : > .
   .rodata                : > .
   .sdata2                : > .
}
```

Figure 46 : GNU Linker Script

The linker generates an elf file. Upon request (-Map option in the linker flags), the linker can also generate a map file which includes the starting address and the size of each section. A map file is very helpful for debugging the code.

It is worth to mention the common definitions of the memory sections:

- .text section – This section holds the software program. This section resides in the flash. After the CPU is powered up, it fetches the instructions from this section in the flash, and starts executing the instructions.
- .data section – The initialized global variables and static local variables. Those variables are modifiable during the run time. After the elf file is loaded to the target, this section resides in the flash. The bootstrap has to copy them from the flash to the RAM during the boot. So, the variables can be modified.
- .bss section – The un-initialized global variables and static local variables. The bootstrap has to initialize this section in the RAM to zeros during the boot.
- .rodata section – The read-only global variables. Since the contents of these variables do not change during the run time, they reside in the flash, and never got moved.

15 .1.3 GNU Debugger

GNU provides "GDB" debugger. The original GDB has no GUI support. It uses the command line interface. Now the GUI version of GDB by the third-party can be found on the market.

15 .2 Load Code to the Target

According to the SECTIONS defined in the linker script file, the executable code image is built. If the code runs in the RAM, IDE tool will load the code to the RAM for testing. If the code runs from the flash, developers have to program the code to the flash (see section 9.2.1). Then reset the CPU, the code can start running without IDE. The code programming can be done by the IDE tool on the host through the JTAG (see section 16.4.3) or SWD (see section 16.4.4).

15 .3 Software Configuration Management Tool (CMT)

CMT helps the developer to track and control the code changes. Every time the developer makes changes to the code, the developer can check the new code into the CMT to preserve the code changes. Sometimes, the developer wants to go back the previous version of code. The developer can retrieve the old version of the code from the CMT.

CMT preserves the version of the code change. At the code release, the build manager can pick up the right code version for the release.

16 Code Implementation

Developing code is easy and fun. But it requires logical mind and disciplines. The developers have to follow the software requirements (either High-Level or Low-Level Requirements) and coding standards. Following the programming rules, the developer translates the requirements into the code. Just write the code according to the requirements, no more no less.

Following the coding standards and making the code clear are important. Clear code is not only for the original developer to retrace the code in the future, but also helps other developers to understand the code easily. Clear code also benefits the reviewer a lot during the code review. The reviewers can follow the logic behind the code. If the code is tangled together, the reviewer will have difficulty to trace the logic of the code.

16 .1 Componentization

With or without RTOS, software should be broken into small components. With the small components, it is easier to implement, to test, and to maintain. In C++ object-oriented programming environment, a class is a building object that holds its own data and functions. Data is encapsuled in the class. It prevents data from being directly accessed by other classes. To access the data in the class from outside needs to go through the provided functions. It is recommended to confine each class in a source file and an include file.

16 .2 Efficient Programming Practices

Due to the limitation of resources, efficient programming is very important for the embedded system. Not only how to manage the memory allocation, also how to make the code run faster. Although this book is not about programming, it is important to mention some programming techniques that can improve the code efficiency:

- Before writing the code for the boot code, device drivers, or firmware, it is important to read the datasheet, the reference manuals, and the programming manual. They provide the information of the processor's architecture, exceptions, the boot procedures, the clock setting, the memory mapping, the memory management, the peripherals, the register setting, … etc. They are very helpful for implementing the low-level code.

- In the virtual addressing environment, the application and the driver code are running in virtual address mode. But for some hardware devices, the physical layer itself may not understand the virtual address. So, when the driver sets the buffer address for the data transfer, it has to convert the virtual address into the physical address, then sets the physical address to the registers or in the buffer descriptors.

- Use compiler -Ox option – The option can reduce the code size or make the code run faster. But be careful, it can eliminate a dummy loop which the developer adds the loop on purpose. To preserve the dummy loop, define the variable of the loop index to be volatile. So, the compiler will keep the code.

- Double or multiple buffering – In a data crunching system, data continues to pour in. If there are more than one buffers, when the data in one buffer is being processed, at the same time, another buffer can be filled with the new data.

- Concurrent processing – If the system has microprocessor/microcontroller, DSP, and DMA, program the devices to be executed simultaneously. For example, the processor can set up DMA, and command the DMA to run. Then the processor can continue with other processing. The processor doesn't need to wait for the DMA to complete. It can check the result later. Or let the DMA completion interrupt inform the processor that the DMA operation is done.

- Table driven – In C/C++ code, the "switch" and "if" statements take more time to do the logical comparison. If possible, use a table for the decision making. When the table stays in the cache, the access time is reduced a lot.

- Exponent of 2 – If a multiplication or division involves in exponent of 2, use the shift operation to do the computation, instead of multiplication or division operation. For some microprocessor or DSP, multiplication and division take more time to complete.

- Use register variables (some newer compiler may not have this option) – In C/C++ languages, variables can be defined as registers. For the frequently used variable, defining it as a register can save a lot of storing and loading time. In this case, the compiler uses a register to hold the value of the variable. Otherwise, the result of the variable will be stored in the memory or cache, and loaded to the register again from the memory or cache when it is needed.

- Use pointer instead of an array – In C/C++ language, the compiler can generate auto-increase address for pointers (i.e., *ptr++) depending on the data type of the variable. If the pointer is defined as "byte", the address will increase by 1. If the pointer is a "word", the address will increase by 4. It needs only one instruction to get the address of the next element. But for the array definition, the compiler has to use the index to compute the offset to the array, and generates the address. It will take many instructions to get the address.

- Consider assembly language – For the time critical inner loop, the efficient assembly code can save a lot of processing time. But it is hard to write the assembly code from scratch. The developer can write the code in C/C++ language first, get the assembly code (with the -S compile option in GCC), and modify the assembly code to become efficient. Be sure to add comments to the assembly code because the assembly code is hard to follow. Good comments can save time in the future.

- Limit memory access – To get data from the memory takes a lot of time. When implementing an algorithm, try to simplify the algorithm to minimize the memory accessing. It can speed up the computation.

- Add "default" to "switch" statement – The "default" option is to handle something not defined in the "switch" statement. It can prevent the unexpected result.
- Access memory sequentially – When processing an array of data, hardware fetches the data to the cache by the cache line. If the data is already in the cache, the CPU does not need to fetch the data from the memory, i.e., processing the data sequentially along the row cells. So, it can save the processing time.
- Static memory allocation – In embedded system, dynamic allocation of memory may cause problems because the memory size is limited, and too many memory allocations and free may cause the memory leak or segmentation. Allocate all the needed memory blocks when the system starts.
- Avoiding recursive calls – Recursive calls may be efficient, but it might cause the stack overflow because the stack size is limited in the embedded system.
- Loop unrolling – Many processors/DSPs have deep pipelining for executing instructions in the CPU. It takes several instructions to fill up the pipeline. Developers may consider using the prologue to prime the pipelines before entering the inner loop, and the epilogue to clear the pipelines after leaving the inner loop.
- Inline function – If a subroutine is short, it can be replaced by an inline function. In this case, instead of making a subroutine call, the compiler will directly insert the code. So, there is no overhead for branching, saving registers to the stack, restoring the registers, and branching back.

16 .3 Common Programming Mistakes

It is easy to make mistakes if a developer doesn't pay attention while programming. Here are some common errors:

- Use uninitialized variables – If a local variable is not initialized, the content of the uninitialized local variable could be anything in the local stack. Sometimes the code works fine, but most of the time, the system crashes.
- Incorrect or out-of-boundary pointer – When a pointer is used for the increment or decrement to access the memory, if the pointer overruns outside the memory boundary, it will wipe out the content of the overrun area. Or a pointer is not initialized, it will be an incorrect pointer. Also, if the index of an array is greater than the defined array size, it will access the area beyond the array.
- Pointer casting – If an array is defined as "char", and a pointer is defined as "int*", cast an array of "char" to the "int" pointer can have two problems. First the alignment, an integer usually has 4-byte boundary alignment. The "char" array might not be allocated on the integer alignment. Second, accessing the "int" pointer is 4 bytes each time, while accessing the "char" array is only one byte each time.
- Size of auto increment – When using auto increment for a pointer (ptr++), depending on the data type of the pointer, the increment of the address varies. For "byte" data type, the increment is one byte a time. For "int" data type, the increment is 4 bytes. If the pointer is a type of data structure, the increment is the size of the data structure.
- Order of operand evaluation – When a statement includes multiple operations, such as +, -, *, /, operations, make sure the order of evaluation by the compiler. It is a good practice to use parentheses to indicate the intended order.
- Stack overflow – A stack is defined for the allocation of the local variables. If the function calls are too deep, and use too much stack space for local variables or arrays, it will wipe out the contents of the overflow area. Some newer processors have hardware to check

the end of the stack. For ARM Cortex-M33, in addition to the stack pointer registers, there are stack limit registers which developers can set up the size of the stack. If the stack pointer is out of the boundary, that will generate an exception.

- Integer overflow – During the arithmetic operation, if the result is larger than the defined capacity (8-bit, 16-bit, 32-bit, or 64-bit), it might cause the bit to wrap around. So, the result is incorrect. For PowerPC, there is an overflow bit in the Integer Exception Register (XER) to indicate an overflow that is caused by the arithmetic operation.

- Copy and paste mistake – When copying and pasting a section of code, make sure to modify the code correctly. Sometimes, a developer just copies and pastes a function, and forgets to make the necessary changes.

- Returning a pointer of a local variable to the calling routine – When the local variables are defined, the contents are stored in the stack. After returning to the calling routine, the area in the stack is released for other use. The content might get changed. So, the contents of a returned pointer in the stack may get changed.

- Checking a floating-point value equal to zero – Although the floating-point variable can represent a huge range of value, it is not very accurate. To compare a floating-point variable to zero may not always work. A floating-Point value can be a very small number, such as 0.00000001, but it is not equal to zero. Also, don't use floating point as the index of the loop or the index to an array.

- Division by zero – If a number is divided by zero, it will cause an exception. For an integer, it is easy to check before the operation to see if the divisor is zero or not. But for a floating point, the divisor can be very small, but not a zero. So, when the code checks whether a divisor is equal to zero or not, it fails to detect the small number.

- English vs Metrix units – Mars Climate Orbiter mission failed in 1999. The failure is due to the fact that one piece of code did not translate the units from English units to Metrix units. Two teams developed two pieces of code separately. One was in English units; the other was in Metrix units. When one of them called the other's functions, the outcome was totally incorrect.

16 .4 Software Debugging

Code debugging should come along with the code developing. After a component is complete, test the code if possible. Don't wait until all components are done, because it is easier to test the code piece by piece, and catch the error earlier. It can prevent re-programming and re-testing the code.

Debugging software needs logic and patience. When something goes wrong, take a deep breath, and find out the patterns. Debugging is not an easy job. It is frustrated when the debugging goes to nowhere. Stop debugging, and take a deep breath, talk to a person, or do something else. Let the mind clear. Then go back and continue the debugging. But repetition can finally reveal some clue.

In Greek mythology, Sisyphus was punished to roll a big boulder up the hill from the bottom. But the boulder rolled down to the bottom when it reached the top. He kept doing this over and over again. If the code is not well designed and developed, fixing bugs just like rolling the boulder. Every time a bug is fixed. But the next bug keeps coming up. The developer needs to spend a tremendous amount of time on fixing the bugs.

Using the debugging tool can help developers to pin point the error in the code. Here is a list of the thoughts and commonly used debugging methods:

16 .4.1 Understanding Schematics and Board Layout

Even for a software developer, understanding the hardware schematics and board layout can contribute a tremendous benefit when it is coming to software debugging. Sometimes, the debugger won't be able to catch what is going on in the hardware. The only way to find out is to use the oscilloscope or the logic analyzer to probe the signals. The developer has to trace those signals by looking at the schematics and board layout, and find the signals and check points to probe.

For example, the processor (master) sends a read request to an I^2C device. But there is no response from the device. The developer checks all the registers and the message. They look fine. The way to find out is checking the signals, Serial Data (SDA) and Serial Clock (SCL) with the oscilloscope. The developer can check the bit pattern of the message (SDA signal), and make sure the message is correct. The developer also can check the clock (SCL signal). Make sure the clock frequency is correct, and see if the clock stays long enough for the I^2C device to send the response back to the processor. Usually, the developer just counts the number of bytes in the transmitting request, and sets the clock only long enough for the transmitting bytes. But the master has to keep the clock running for receiving the return value. So, the master can receive the return bytes.

If there are check points for the desired signals, it is not difficult to probe the signals with the oscilloscope. If not, the developer can trace the signals from the processor to the device, and find a appropriate point to probe, such as a pin or a resistor. Nowadays, all the chips are so small, and the chips are mounted on the surface of the PC board. To check a single pin on the chip is difficult and dangerous because that pin might be next to a power pin. If the probe slips and touches the power pin at the same time, it might damage the chip. The best way is to add a wire to the pin and clip on the wire.

16 .4.2 Understanding Assembly Language

Nowadays only few developers write code in assembly language. The language is not structured. It is very difficult to develop, debug and maintain. But during the debugging, the tools may show the code in the assembly language. So, the developer can step into the assembly instructions. It is very useful to look at the contents of the registers/memory, and to see how the values get changed. It helps the developers to discover the unexpected value in the register/memory. Sometimes, the developer can modify the content of the register/memory to avoid the crash, and continue debugging the code.

16 .4.3 Joint Test Access Group (JTAG)

JTAG specifies the use of a dedicated debug port that implements a serial communication interface for low-overhead access to the on-board chips, such as processors, DSP, and memory. It does not need the direct access to the processor's external address and data buses. The interface connects to an on-chip test access port which includes 5 major lines: Test Clock, Test Mode Select, Test Input, Test Output, and Test Reset. The input line and the output line are separate. The port sends proper signal sequences to access a set of test registers on the chip.

16 .4.4 Serial Wire Debug (SWD)

SWD replaces the 5-pin JTAG port with a clock pin (SWCLK) and a bi-directional data pin (SWDIO). But it still uses JTAG protocol. Since it requires only two pins, it is widely used in the chips that have pin-limited package, such as ARM Cortex-M processors. Like the JTAG's debug and test capability, SWD provides a special function that can access the system memory and internal registers in real-time.

SWD can pass data between the debugger on the host and the target system efficiently. Since the serial data bus (SWDIO) is bi-directional, to avoid data collision, there are three phases for data transmitting: Packet Request, Acknowledge Response, and Data Transfer. The standard protocol of SWD passing data is well defined in ARM Debug Interface v5. Many ARM processor company's IDE tools (such as NXP MCUXpresso) have adopted the standard interface.

16 .4.5 In-Circuit Emulator (ICE)

The in-circuit emulator is a piece of hardware that works with JTAG/SWD. Either the chip maker or the third party (such as Lauterbach, Wind River, or QEMU) builds the hardware emulator and the debugger on top of the JTAG/SWD. The hardware emulator allows the developer to debug the code at real-time. Many microprocessors and DSPs provide the JTAG/SWD port. One end of an emulator probe is connected to the port on the target board. The other end of the probe is connected to the host (PC) by USB cable or Ethernet cable. The debugger tool runs on the host.

ICE programmers are not only used for debugging purpose, it also used to write code and data into the flash memory on the target. For the memory chip that provides the JTAG/SWD interface, the programmer tool can write the built code/data directly to the flash. Otherwise, writing to the flash needs to use processor's data bus.

16 .4.6 Debugger

A debugger or debugging tool is a piece of software program that is running on the host. It can communicate with the target system through JTAG, SWD ports or some other mechanisms. The developer can set breakpoints, step through the C/C++ code with symbols or the assembly code without symbols, look into the memory, the registers, … etc.

Generally, a debugger just takes care of memory and registers. It does not know the RTOS. In order to work with RTOS, the debugger needs RTOS-aware debugging which allows the developer to look into RTOS's task information, mutexes, semaphores, messages in the mailbox, the CPU budget usage, and the usage of stack. Not all debugger has RTOS-aware debugging capability. Developers have to check with the debugger provider to find out whether the debugger has the RTOS-aware debugging capability or not.

For some processor, in addition to the software breakpoints, the developer can set hardware breakpoints in the debugger. Hardware breakpoint responds faster than software breakpoint because hardware breakpoint uses special registers and has less overhead. It can catch some important events. But it is not as flexible as the software breakpoint. Usually, the developer can set many software breakpoints, but only one or two hardware breakpoints. It is depending on the processor.

The debugger uses the concept of "trap" which causes the program to stop. A trap can be an illegal instruction that generates an exception. When the developer sets a software breakpoint at an instruction or at an address, the debugger temporarily replaces the instruction at the location with an illegal instruction, such as "BKPT" instruction in ARM instruction set. When the CPU hits the illegal instruction, it stops execution. In IDE environment, the debugger then displays the source code at that location if the code is built with debug symbols (i.e. -g option in GNU compiler). If the built code has no symbols, it displays the assembly code.

At the break point, the developer can query the processor to read the memory, the registers, or inspect variables, data structures, the call stack in IDE. Either in C/C++ code or in assembly code, the developer can run the program step by step, step into a subroutine, step over a subroutine, or run through a subroutine till the return. In some cases, the developer can change the address of the execution (alter the value in the Program Counter Register) to avoid the instructions that cause the system to crash.

16 .4.7 Simulator

Simulator is a software tool for debugging software. When the hardware is not ready for use, software engineer can use the simulator to debug the code. For example, TI DSP has simulator in Code Composer Studio (CCS) for the DSP and the processor. When the TI DSP host board is not ready, software engineers can use TI CCS simulator to test the code.

16 .4.8 Serial Output

Sometimes there is no debugging tool from the chip maker or the third party. Or in order to catch the bug, the code needs to run continuously, and cannot use breakpoints. The common debugging practice is to output the results from the serial port of the target to COM port on the host (PC). The serial connection can be UART or Ethernet. The UART output messages can be displayed on the console through the COM port on PC. For ARM Cortex-M processor, SWD replaces the traditional UART connection. The output from the target system is displayed in the console window in IDE environment.

For UART communication, the target needs the serial port pin connector from the processor. Usually, the connector includes only few signals (Tx, Rx, ground pins) from the processor (see section 6.3). The application sends the message out through something like "printf" statement. The host uses "HyperTerminal" to receive the message on the COM port and display them on the screen. Nowadays new PCs don't support the 9-pin COM port connector. Instead, the new PC provides the USB ports, and the "Serial to USB" adapter which replaces the UART connector on the PC.

For the Ethernet connection, it is more complicated. On the target, the developer needs the Ethernet port and software to build the Ethernet packages. On the PC side, it needs an Ethernet port and a network protocol analyzer to receive and display the packages on the screen. There are several applications on the market, such as Network Analyzer Sniffer Tools. Sometimes there is only one or no Ethernet port on the PC, and this Ethernet port is used for the wired network connection. Instead of Ethernet port, USB ports are popular on the PC. It is not hard to find "Ethernet to USB" adapters on the market.

16 .5 Unit Test

Each developer needs to test individual's code, and to make sure the code is bug free and meets the requirement. It is easier to test the code individually than to test the whole code altogether. The developer can find its own bugs without other developer's interference. Unit test will ease the integration test in the future.

16 .6 Check-in the Code

During the code implementation, when the developer feels the code is working or the code is worth of saving, it is time to save the code in the Configuration Management Tool (CMT) before the code gets modified or lost. Although the developer can recover or rewrite the lost code without CMT, it is wasting time and frustrating. So, depending on the developer's comfortable level, code should be saved time to time. The checked-in code must be free of compile error because other developer may check out the code from CMT and build the code for testing. The process of building the code may take a long time. It is waste of time if the code cannot be built.

But when integrating with other developers, the developer has to pay a lot of more attention when checking the code into the Configuration Management Tool. Not only the code has no compile error, but also it won't crash the system. At the integration phase, to build the whole system may take a long time. Sometimes, building the whole system is undergoing through the night. If something fails, many developers cannot continue their job next morning. Developers have to double check their code, and make sure the code is working before checking the code into the Configuration Management Tool.

16 .7 Requirement Traceability

For each subroutine, it should be able to trace back to one of the software requirements, either High-Level Requirement or Low-Level Requirement. For the code that is not in the requirement (called dead code) should be removed. Although the developer thinks it is harmless, it might cause problem in the future. From the history of spacecraft, the harmless code did cause the space mission to fail.

16 .8 Software Code Review

Software code review is important. Not only it can detect the bugs, also it helps other developers to understand the code. It has the following benefits:

- Check whether the code is vulnerable to the attacks from the hackers.
- Check whether the code meets the coding standards. Some company has the coding standards. So, the code is neat and clean. It is easier to read.
- Check whether the code meets the requirements. Software code shall do exactly as the software requirements state, no more no less.
- Check the logic of the algorithm implementations. Make sure the algorithm is implemented correctly. If the code is written according to the coding standards, the reviewer can easily follow the logic.
- Catch the software bugs in the early stage. It is easier to fix the bug if the bug is found earlier.
- More engineers to understand the code. So, the developers other than the original author can pick up the code quickly. Usually, the original developers move to another project when the project is released. Most of them won't stay in the same project after the release.

17 Booting Process

When the processor is powered on or cold reset, the power-on-reset signal (active low) is asserted. After the power ramps up to a certain stable level, the processor waits for several more clock cycles (depending on the processor). It then desserts the power-on-reset signal (bring the signal to high). So, the processor is out of reset. It waits for another certain clock cycles, then starts initializing the whole processor.

After the PLL is locked, the processor checks the boot mode. For ARM Cortex-M, the processor reads BOOT0 and BOOT1 pins to determine the boot mode. For PowerPC MPC8280, the processor checks MODCK [1-3] pins to determine the boot mode.

For ARM Cortex-M processor, the CPU then fetches the End-of-Stack address from the beginning of the interrupt vector table (see section 4.4.1), and places the pointer in the stack pointer register (SP or R13). Next step, the CPU reads the starting address of the boot code from the second entry (offset 0x04) of the interrupt vector table, stores the address in program counter register (PC or R15), and starts to execute the boot code.

For PowerPC MPC8280, the processor reads four bytes of the Hard Reset Configuration Word (HRCW) from the flash memory which is tied to chip select 0. Since the registers of chip select 0 is not programmed at the moment, the processor uses the slower speed to read those four bytes one by one. From the HRCW, the processor then figures out where to get the interrupt vector table, fetch the start address of the boot code from the table, and starts to execute the boot code. Since the processor does not put the End-of-Stack in the stack pointer register (SP or R13), the bootstrap code has to program the SP register.

Now the hardware has done its job, the bootstrap code starts to run. Generally, for the embedded system, the application code already resides in the flash memory. There is no need to load the application code from other device. Most of the time, the bootstrap code does not get changed. But the application code may change from time to time.

There are a lot of system registers need be set up by the bootstrap, including the chip select registers for the flash memory and RAM, SIU, PLL, ... etc. The bootstrap also performs the RAM test. After the registers are set, and RAM is tested, the bootstrap checks the integrity of the application code in the flash. Usually there are 2 copies of the application code in the flash. One is the most recent (current) copy, the other is the copy of previous application code. If the current copy is corrupted (either CRC error or decryption fail) or not working correctly, bootstrap can switch back to the previous copy, and run the old version of the application code.

If the application code is good, depending on the requirements, the application code may stay in the flash memory. The CPU executes the application code from the flash memory. For others, the application code may be copied from the flash memory to the RAM for faster execution. After the application code is copied, the bootstrap branches to the main function in the application code if there is no RTOS. If the RTOS is involved, the bootstrap copies the RTOS from the flash memory to RAM, and passes the control to the RTOS.

17.1 Secure Boot

Secure boot is a mechanism for ensuring the integrity of the bootloader, the application code, the operating system, and the signature data. It enables the system to guard against the attacking, or unauthorized software updating.

One feature of Secure Boot mechanism is to use public/private key encryption (see section 21). The firmware, application code, operation system and the signature data are encrypted with the private key(s) that only the originator has the key(s). For different code may use different pair of encryption and decryption key. The bootstrap keeps the public key(s) of the code and the data in an isolated place, and prevents the public key(s) from alternation. Before handing over the control to the application code/RTOS, the bootstrap uses the public key(s) to check the integrity of the code and the data. It is nearly impossible for the hacker to know the private key. So, if the unauthorized code is loaded to the flash, it won't pass the checking.

Also, the bootstrap code itself and the signature data can be secured by hardware. Some flash memory reserves a sector or sectors as protected section. Without the physical hardware setup, this section of the flash is not writable. The bootstrap code and data can be stored in this section. So, the bootstrap code is secured.

17 .2 Bootloader

Bootloader is a piece of code that loads the operating system, or the application code. After the bootstrap complete its own task, if necessary, the bootloader copies the operating system or the application code to the RAM, and passes the control to the operating system or the application code.

When the code or data in the flash is corrupted, the bootloader can download the code from other sources, such as multi-media, the USB flash drive, or the network. The download process can be guarded by another set of the public/private keys. Bootloader will check the source of the new code. Only the authorized party can send the code to the target.

18 Verification and Validation

According to the requirements, hardware and software shall be tested independently according to Hardware Requirements and Software Requirements (both High-level and Low-level). After both have been fully tested, the whole system shall be tested according to the System Requirements.

18 .1 Formal Release Build

Before conducting a formal test, not only software needs a formal release, hardware also needs to make a formal release. When the time is ready for release, the developers check in their code to the Configuration Management Tool (CMT). The build manager tags all the files that will be in this release with a name, and copies out those files to the build area, then builds the formal release. So, it is clear which files are included in the release.

For each release of the product, a unique version number is assigned to the release. Depending on the severity of the bug or improvement (Major, Minor, or Patch), the version number can be assigned differently. The build manager updates the software version and hardware revision numbers in version control file. Then the manager builds the official release. Hardware revision number is important, because the hardware changes could require the software change, too. In order to match the code and the hardware, both numbers must be listed in the version control file which is loaded to the flash memory.

The version number could have a set of 3 numbers. Each number represents Major, Minor, or Patch.

- When there is a major release, the Major number is increased by 1, and the Minor and the Patch numbers are reset.
- When the release is minor, keep the Major number, increase the Minor number by 1, and reset the Patch number.
- If the release is a patch, keep the Major and Minor numbers intact, and increase the Patch number by 1.

The software version number is embedded in the version control file and inside the code. After boot up, the application code can check the version number in the code against the number in the flash memory. The application code also verifies the software version numbers and the hardware revision number to make sure they match each other. If they don't match, the new release is not valid, and stops further executing.

The hardware revision number is printed on the circuit board. It is visible to a person or the machine.

18 .2 Loading the Code to the Target

The boot code and the application code have different release images. Follow the procedures to load them separately to the target. Usually, the boot code doesn't get updated. It is loaded during the manufacturing. The application also loaded during the manufacturing, but it can be updated in the future.

18 .3 Hardware Test

To ensure hardware meets the requirements, hardware test is performed on the released hardware. If software is required for the hardware test, use the officially released software. Depends on the product, some products require to operate in extreme environments, such below frozen temperature, high heat temperature, radiation, electromagnetic Interference, or lightning strikes.

18 .3.1 Temperature Test

Put the hardware in a chamber to make sure the hardware is still working at very high or very low temperatures. The test can be determined by the output that is generated by software through the UART output.

18 .3.2 Lightning Strike Test

Apply the high voltage to the hardware to make sure the hardware still functioning under or after this condition. During the test, check the UART output to see the irregularity.

This test is one of the requirements for the avionic navigation system. The airplane might be hit by the lightning. The test can prove that the navigation system still works after the lightning hit.

18 .3.3 Electromagnetic Interference (EMI) Test

Emissions testing (also called Interference Testing) involves in measuring the electromagnetic signals that are unintentionally emitted by the equipment under the test. It is to determine if these emissions exceed the permissible limits. Excessive emissions could potentially cause problems for other nearby devices.

18 .4 Software Verification and Validation

In a large scale of code development, when the individual developer finishes the code, it is time to integrate with other developer's code. Software integration test can be done module by module. Don't wait until all the modules are done, then perform the integration test. At that time, there is too much code to pin point the failure because it is just too complicated.

18 .4.1 Verification

The process of verification is to trace from the requirement to design and finally to code. It verifies whether the requirements are all covered by the design and the code. Also trace back from the code to design and the requirement to make sure there is no extra code. This process is done by inspection and analysis for small and simple systems. The developers trace from the software requirements to design and then to the code, and vice versa.

For large and complicated systems, in addition to inspection and analysis, the developers can use the requirements management tool to make the traces, such as Rational DOORS by IBM. For each requirement in the High-Level Software Requirements document, the tool can make a link to the requirement in the Low-Level Software Requirements or to the function calls in the code. The tool also can trace backward from the code all ways to the High-Level Software Requirements.

18 .4.2 Validation

The product has been built according to the requirements, but does it work? The developers need to validate that the product works. Validation process is to make sure the code is doing what it supposed to do, and the code has accomplished the goal of the requirements. To prove it, the test engineers write the test code. The tests can be performed in Black-Box test and White-Box test (see section 3.4.2). The test code covers each requirement, and generates the test report to prove the code is working. For some inevitable obstacles, some requirements are not able to be tested. The code can be justified by inspections.

18 .5 System Verification and Validation

This is the integration test for testing hardware and software together. A test plan is written to describe the test cases against the system requirements. According to the test cases, the test engineers write the test code to verify and validate the whole system.

19 Maintenance

Remember: software update is inevitable. Although the product has been delivered, the job is not quite completely done yet. In the field, the customer may find some bugs or have new requirements, or there is something need be improved. So, the job will keep going for a while.

For the long-haul product, some component might be no longer in production, and a new component replace the old component. In evidently hardware need be updated and re-spin. Test engineers have to conduct the hardware test again. If software need be updated, too, the updated software must be tested again (regression test). Even if there is no software change, the whole system still needs be tested.

The maintenance job is boring, but it is still very important. The original developer/engineer may already leave the company or be assigned to another project. Whoever picks up the task relies on the document, and the code. If the code was written according to coding standard, the new developer can easily understand the logic of code. Coding standard is not a guideline. It is one of the requirements in the embedded system.

20 Mechanical Design

Unlike hardware design and software design, mechanical design does not involve the electronics. But it is still important for the embedded system, especially the consumer products. When people look at a product, they see only the outside shape of the product. The circuit board and software are hidden behind the shell.

Mechanical design involves in putting hardware together in a box. It also needs to leave the communication ports open. So, the product can communicate with other devices. There are some considerations while designing the mechanism of the system:

- Security – To protect the product against the hacker, some mechanical component can be implemented with the electronic component for the product. For example, when the box of the device is opened by the unauthorized party, the alarm goes off or the device stops working. So, the hacker won't be able to steal the information in the box.
- Meet the requirements – For the product that the customer provides the specifications, the product has to meet the shape, the size and the weight of the requirements. Here is an example: the airplane manufacturer asks the supplier to build the LRU (Line Replaceable Unit), such as the navigation system or the radar system. It gives the supplier the specifications about the shape, the size, and the maximum weight of the product because the size and the weight are very important for the airplane.
- Hessel-free assembly – To assemble the product in the factory plays an important role in the manufacturing cost. A good mechanical design can save the assembling time and reduce the cost.
- EMI protection – Some circuits may generate the EMI which can impact other sensitive device's function. A metallic shield can be made to cover the circuits. The shield absorbs the EMI and prevents the EMI from leaking.
- The appearance – Appearance is important for a product, especially for the consumer products. If the appearance of the product is appealing, the customer may feel more willing to buy the product.

21 RSA Public-Key Cryptosystems

In 1978, three scientists, Dr. Ron Rivest, Dr. Adi Shamir, and Dr. Leonard Adleman, at MIT published the RSA Public-Key Cryptosystems which is named by the initials of their last names. For the conventional cryptosystems, both encryption and decryption keys must be kept secret. The sender and the receiver need to know both keys. To deliver those keys may become a problem. They might get intercepted during the delivery.

In the public-key cryptosystem which is an asymmetric cryptosystem, the encryption and the description are governed by two distinct keys: the encryption key and the decryption key. The encryption key can be publicly disclosed. But the decryption key is private. Only the receiver knows the decryption key. Anyone can use the public (encryption) key to send an encrypted message to the receiver, and only the intended receiver can decrypt the message. The receiver can change the pair of the keys at any time to prevent the old keys being hacked.

Another advantage of the Public-Key Cryptosystem is allowing the sender to sign an electronic mail. Since anyone can send the message to the receiver, some messages might be fake. The sender can sign the electronic mail by encrypting the ciphered message again, i.e., the ciphered message is encrypted again by the sender's private decryption key. The receiver first uses the sender's public encryption key to decipher the received message, then uses the receiver's own private decryption key to retrieve the original message.

21 .1 The Properties

The properties of the RSA Public-Key cryptosystem are:

1. The public key is a pair of positive integers (e, n).
2. The message M must be a number between 0 and (n-1). When sending the text message, each character can be converted to ASCII code or Unicode which are numbers. Or each character is converted into a smaller number (see the example in section 21.4).

   $$0 < M < (n-1)$$

3. The encryption procedure raises the message (M) to the power of the encryption key (e), and then mod n. The remainder of the modulo operation is the ciphered message (M').

   $$M' = E(M) = (M)^e \bmod n$$

4. The decryption key is another pair of positive integers, (d, n), where n is the same as the n in the encryption key pair (e, n). The procedure of decryption of a ciphered message is the inverse of the encryption procedure. The ciphered message is raised to the power of the decryption key (d), and then mod n. The remainder of the modulo operation is the original message.

   $$M = D(M') = (M')^d \bmod n$$

The cryptosystem is well secured because the integers used are very large. It will take years to find out the relationship between the encryption key and the decryption key.

The sender can further sign the message by adding another layer of encryption to the already ciphered message. The encryption key and the decryption key are complementary. In step 3, the decryption key (*d, n*) of the sender is used to encrypt the already ciphered message (M'). The signed ciphered message (S') is sent to the receiver.

$S' = E(M') = (M')^d \bmod n$, where S' is the signed ciphered message, and (*d, n*) is the sender's private decryption key pair.

The receiver first uses the sender's public encryption key (*e, n*) to obtain the ciphered message (M'). Then the receiver follows the step 4 to retrieve the original message (M).

$M' = D(S') = (S')^e \bmod n$, where (e, n) is the sender's public key pair.

$M = D(M') = (M')^d \bmod n$, where (d, n) is the receiver's decryption key pair.

21 .2 Finding the Keys

The RSA Cryptosystem is based on the large prime numbers. Here are the procedures to find the encryption and decryption keys:

- Find two large prime numbers, p and q. Each can be 256 bits or larger. First, use the random number to generate a number, p. Check whether the generated number, p, is a prime number or not. If there is no Hardware Random Number Generator (HRNG) in the processor, the algorithm in section 21.3.1 can generate a prime number. Find q with the same method. Both p and q must be different numbers, i.e., p is not equal to q.
- Calculating, n and ϕ, where n is used in the encryption key (e, n) and decryption key (d, n).

  $n = p * q$

  $\phi = (p - 1) * (q - 1)$

  where n is 512 bits if p and q each has 128 bits.
- Finding the decryption key, d which can be randomly generated. But the decryption key must have the following properties:
  - d must be a number greater than p and q, but less than ϕ.
  - And gcd(d, ϕ) = 1 where gcd stands for greatest common divisor. If d is a prime number, then d satisfies this property.

- Finding the encryption key, e which is the multiplicative inverse of d. To compute e, use the Extended Euclidean Algorithm (see section 21.3.2):

  $(e * d) \bmod \phi = 1$

  where e must be a positive integer
- For e and d keys, they are exchangeable. After finding both keys, e and d, if encryption key e is larger than decryption key d, swap encryption key and decryption key to make it harder to find the decryption key. Both keys must be tested to make sure they are working before making the encryption key (e, n) public.

21.3 Practical Algorithms

In order to improve the security, large numbers are used in the computation. The larger the numbers, the more secure of the cryptosystem. But due to the limitation of the computer, the largest number can be stored in a 32-bit word is $2^{31} - 1$, which is about 10 decimal digits, or a 64-bit double word is $2^{63} - 1$, which is about 19 decimal digits. Here the numbers are at least 256 bits each. The regular mathematical operations $(+, -, *, /, \text{mod})$ are not able to handle such large numbers. New algorithms are needed to solve the problems.

21 .3.1 Finding Prime Number and Primality Test

In section 21.2, those two numbers, p and q, must be prime numbers and not be equal. Those numbers are randomly generated. Testing of primality of a randomly generated number is not easy. There are many methods to test the primality of a number. Each method has its own advantages and disadvantages. None of them can definitely confirm that a randomly generated number is prime.

In[1], the Algorithm P (Probabilistic Primality Test) provides a method to generate a random number, and test the primality of the number.

1. Let $P = 1 + 2^k * d$, where k and d are random positive integers, and d is an odd number.
2. Generate another random integer, X, that $1 < X < P$.
3. Set j = 0;
   $m = 2^j$;
   $Y = X^{m*d} \bmod P$;
4. If ((j == 0) and (Y == 1)) or if (Y == (P – 1)) then terminate and go to step 7.
5. If ((j > 0) and (Y == 1)), then terminate and go to step 8.
6. Set j = j + 1;
   Set $Y = Y^2 \bmod P$;
   If (j < k), go to step 4, else go to step 8.
7. P is probably prime.
8. P is definitely not prime.

According to the test, this method will be wrong at most ¼ of the time for P. In order to decrease the possibility of failure, X can be independently generated 10 or 20 times. For 10 times, the probability of failure will become $(1/4)^{10}$, which is very small possibility of failure.

21 .3.2 Extended Euclidean Algorithm

To find the encryption key e (the multiplicative inverse of decryption key d), the Extended Euclidean Algorithm in [1] can be implemented as follows:

$$(e * d) \bmod \phi = 1$$

Pseudo code:

```
Set u1 = 1; u3 = d;
Set v1 = 0; v3 = φ;
While (v3 != 0) do
Begin
    x = u3 / v3;
    y1 = u1 – (v1 * x);
    y3 = u3 – (v3 * x);
    u1 = v1;
    u3 = v3;
    v1 = y1;
    v3 = y3;
end
Finally, e = u1;
If e < 0; then e = e + φ;
```

21.3.3 Binary Powering Algorithm

When trying to encrypt the message, the message is raised to the power of encryption key e and then mod by n, i.e.

$$M' = (M)^e \bmod n$$

Since e is a huge number, say 256 bits, it is not practical to directly raise M to the power of e, then mod with n. Instead, the Binary Powering Algorithm in [1] can ease the computation. This algorithm also applies to decryption of the message, $M = (M')^d \bmod n$. Here is how the algorithm works:

From the example in section 21.4, the public key e is $17 = 0x11 = (10001)_2$. Convert the exponent e into a binary representation:

$$e = 17_{10} = (1 \quad 0 \quad 0 \quad 0 \quad 1)_2$$
$$\phantom{e = 17_{10} = (} e_k \quad e_{k-1} \quad e_{k-2} \quad \cdots \quad e_0$$

Pseudo code:

```
Let C = 1;
For j = k downto 0 do
Begin
    Set C = C² mod n;
    If(e_j == 1)
    Begin
        Set C = (M * C) mod n;
    End
    --j;
End
```

Finally, C is the result of $(M)^e \bmod n$.

21 .3.4 Division of Non-negative Integers

Since the numbers are huge integers, they won't be able to fit in a word or a double word. They have to be stored in the integer arrays. To do the division of the arrays needs a special function. In [1], the Algorithm D (Division of Non-negative Integers) reveals an easier way to perform the operation.

Given two non-negative integer arrays,

$U = (U_{m+n-1} \cdots U_1 U_0)_b$ and

$V = (V_{n-1} \cdots V_1 V_0)_b$,

where b is the base which can be 10, 16, 32 … etc., V_{n-1} != 0, and n > 1.
The quotient is $Q = U/V = (Q_m Q_{m-1} \cdots Q_1 Q_0)_b$ and the remainder is $R = U \bmod V$ $= (R_{n-1} \cdots R_1 R_0)_b$. Then the steps of the division are as follows:

1. Let $d = b/(V_{n-1} + 1)$

    Set $(U_{m+n} U_{m+n-1} \cdots U_1 U_0)_b =$
    $(U_{m+n-1} \cdots U_1 U_0)_b * d$
    where a new digit position, U_{m+n}, might be introduced to the left of U_{m+n-1}. If the result of $(d * U_{m+n-1})$ is greater than b or equal to b, the new digit will be introduced.

    Set $(V_{n-1} \cdots V_1 V_0)_b = (V_{n-1} \cdots V_1 V_0)_b * d$
    Since d is always less than b/2, the result of $(d * V_{n-1})$ is less than b. In this case, there is no new digit is introduced.

2. Set j = m;

3. Set $q = ((U_{j+n} * b) + U_{j+n-1}) / V_{n-1}$;

    Set $r = ((U_{j+n} * b) + U_{j+n-1}) \bmod V_{n-1}$;

    If $(q == b)$ or $((q * V_{n-2}) > ((b * r) + U_{j+n-2}))$, then q = q - 1, and r = r + V_{n-1}; repeat this "if" test until both tests are no longer true.

4. Set $(U_{j+n} U_{j+n-1} \cdots U_j)_b = (U_{j+n} U_{j+n-1} \cdots U_j)_b - (q * (V_{n-1} \cdots V_1 V_0)_b)$
    If the result is negative, go to step 6.

5. Set $Q_j = q$, go to step 7.

6. Set $Q_j = q - 1$ and add $(0 V_{n-1} \cdots V_1 V_0)_b$ back to $(U_{j+n} U_{j+n-1} \cdots U_j)_b$

7. j = j -1. If j >= 0, go back to step 3.

8. Now $(Q_m Q_{m-1} \ldots Q_1 Q_0)_b$ is the desired quotient, and the desired remainder can be obtained by $(U_{n-1} \ldots U_1 U_0)_b / d$.

21 .4 A Simple Example

Here is a very simple example:

Let p = 47

q = 61

n = p * q = 47 * 61 = 2867

ɸ = (p – 1) * (q – 1) = (47 – 1) * (61 – 1) = 46 * 60 = 2760

Choose d = 2273 which is greater than p and q, but less than ɸ. It is a prime number.

The decryption key d is equal to 2273 and ɸ is equal to 2760. So, (e * 2273) mod 2760 = 1. Use the Extended Euclidean Algorithm to find the encryption key:

(e * d) mod ɸ = 1, i.e. (e * 2273) mod 2760 = 1

Find e = 17

The public encryption key is (17, 2867), and the private decryption key is (2273, 2867). To send a character string:

"IT IS A SECRET"

Remember, the message (M) must be satisfied with 0 < M < (2867 – 1). In order to meet M < (2867 – 1), each character is converted into a number from 0 to 26. For space = 00, A = 01, B = 02, ... Y = 25, Z = 26. Therefore, 2 characters can be sent together because the largest number of 2 characters (ZZ) is 2626 which is less than (2867 – 1). Here is the look-up table:

sp	00	C	03	F	06	I	09	L	12	O	15	R	18	U	21	X	24
A	01	D	04	G	07	J	10	M	13	P	16	S	19	V	22	Y	25
B	02	E	05	H	08	K	11	N	14	Q	17	T	20	W	23	Z	26

Figure 47: Character Convert Table

The message string is converted to:

0920 0009 1900 0100 1905 0318 0520

First, send the first 2 characters, "IT". The ciphered message, M' = (M)^e mod n.

So, $M' = (920)^{17}$ mod $2867 = 2781$. The ciphered message, 2781, is sent to the receiver.

The receiver then uses his own decryption key, d, to decipher the message by
$M = (M')^{d}$ mod n.
So, $M = (2781)^{2273}$ mod $2867 = 920$. The receiver gets the 2 characters, "IT".

Next, send the following 2 characters, " I":
$M' = (9)^{17}$ mod $2867 = 1179$. The ciphered message, 1179, is sent to the receiver.
To decipher the message:
$M = (1179)^{2273}$ mod $2867 = 9$, i.e. $0009 = $ " I".
...
...
Finally, send the last 2 characters, "ET":
$M' = (520)^{17}$ mod $2867 = 284$. The ciphered message, 284, is sent to the receiver.
To decipher the message:
$M = (284)^{2273}$ mod $2867 = 520$.

This is a very simple example. When the number (n) gets very big, more characters can be sent in a message, as long as, the message (M) satisfies, $0 < M < (n-1)$.

22 Advanced Encryption Standard (AES)

AES was developed by Vincent Rijmen and Joan Daemen in 1998, and adopted by US government in 2001. Now it is widely spread throughout the world. Many SoCs provide the AES engine to accelerate the cryptographic process. It is the symmetric block cypher which means the same key is used for data encryption and decryption.

Since both sides need to use the same AES key, the key has to be transferred from one side to the other side(s). It becomes vulnerable that the key may be intercepted during transfer. To avoid the key from being intercepted, the key can be delivered by using RSA Public Key cryptography. The sender can encrypt the AES key by using the receiver's public encryption key, and the sender's own decryption key (see section 21.1). Then the signed encrypted AES key is sent to the receiver. On the receiver's side, first the receiver uses the sender's public encryption key to decrypt the message, then uses the receiver's own decryption key to decrypt the message to get the AES key.

Comparing to the RSA Public Key Cryptosystem, AES has better performance. Since e, d, and n in RSA cryptosystem are large numbers, to compute "$(M)^e$ mod n" or "$(M')^d$ mod n" would involves intensive multiplication and modulo operations, especially the decryption because the private key is larger than the public key.

22 .1 AES Properties

Here are the features of AES:

- The length of the message is fixed at 128 bits (16 bytes in one dimensional array). If the message is less than 128 bits, add paddings to make it up to 128 bits. The 128-bit (16-byte) message is rearranged in a 4 x 4 state array. The first byte is put at the array index [0][0]. The second byte is at [1][0]. The third byte is at [2][0], and so on.

Message; {byte0, byte1, byte2, byte3, byte4, byte5, byte6, byte7, byte8, byte9, byte10, byte11, byte12, byte13, byte14, byte15}

State Array

byte0	byte4	byte8	byte12
byte1	byte5	byte9	byte13
byte2	byte6	byte10	byte14
byte3	byte7	byte11	byte15

Figure 48 : 4 x 4 State Array

- The cypher key can be randomly generated. AES supports 3 different lengths of the cypher key: 128-bit, 192-bit, and 256-bit.
- The number of rounds for transformation is 10 rounds for 128-bit cypher key, 12 rounds for 192-bit cypher key, and 14 rounds for 256-bit cypher key.

	Key Length (in bytes)	Key Length (Nk words)	Block Size (Nb words)	Number of Rounds (Nr)
128-bit	16	4	4	10
192-bit	24	6	4	12
256-bit	32	8	4	14

Figure 49 : Summary of Key, Block and Round

- The cypher key is expanded into the round key schedule.
- For encryption and decryption, the AES algorithm of transformations is performed in each round. Except the last round which

doesn't include the column mixing function, the following trans-formation functions are processed in each round:

1. Byte Substitution
2. Row Shifting
3. Column Mixing
4. Adding a Round Key

- Before the round processing loop, there is a pre-round transform-ation which is not included in the round processing loop. The pre-round performs only the "Adding a Round Key" transformation. Therefore, the number of sets for the round key schedule is 11 (pre-round + 10 round) sets for 128-bit, 13 (pre-round + 12 round) sets for 192-bit, and 15 (pre-round + 14 round) sets for 256-bit. Each set is 4 words. So, the length of the round key schedule is 44 words for 128-bit, 52 words for 192-bit, and 60 words for 256-bit.
- The processing in each round has an input state array and generate an output state array.

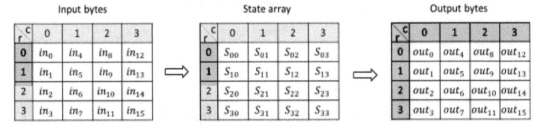

Figure 50: State Array Input and Output

- The output of the encryption is a 128-bit cyphered message, and the output of the decryption is the original 128-bit message.

22 .2 AES Algorithms

The algorithms used by AES include SubBytes, ShiftRows, MixColumns, and AddRoundKey. Most of the mathematical computation is performed in finite field.

22 .2.1 Finite Field Computation

Finite field computation is different from the number computation. Here are the commonly used operations:

- Addition and subtraction (denoted by $\oplus$) – Both addition and subtraction in finite field are performed with XOR operation. They are bit wise XORing.
- Division (denoted by /) – Finite field can be represented in the polynomial form. First convert the bit field into polynomial. Then use the polynomial division to get the quotient and the remainder. The results are converted back to the bit field.
- Multiplication (denoted by •) – Use the polynomial multiplication with the modulo of the irreducible polynomial of degree 8 ($X^8 + X^4 + X^3 + X + 1$). The remainder of the modulo becomes the product of the multiplication. For example:

  $\{0x91\} \bullet \{0x37\}$
  $= \{1\,0\,0\,1\,0\,0\,0\,1\} \bullet \{0\,0\,1\,1\,0\,1\,1\,1\}$
  $\{0x91\} = X^7 + X^4 + 1$
  $\{0x37\} = X^5 + X^4 + X^2 + X + 1$
  $(X^7 + X^4 + 1) \bullet (X^5 + X^4 + X^2 + X + 1)$
  $= (X^{12} + X^{11} + X^7 + X^6 + X^2 + X + 1)$
  Then $(X^{12} + X^{11} + X^7 + X^6 + X^2 + X + 1) /$
  $(X^8 + X^4 + X^3 + X + 1) = X^4 + X^3 + 1$,
  And the remainder: $X^7 + X^5 + X^4 + X^2$
  Therefore, $\{0x91\} \bullet \{0x37\}$
  $= \{1\,0\,0\,1\,0\,0\,0\,1\} \bullet \{0\,0\,1\,1\,0\,1\,1\,1\}$
  $= \{1\,1\,0\,0\,0\,1\,1\,0\,0\,0\,1\,1\,1\} / \{1\,0\,0\,0\,1\,1\,0\,1\,1\}$
  $= \{1\,1\,0\,0\,1\}$, and the remainder:
  $\{1\,0\,1\,1\,0\,1\,0\,0\} = 0xB4$
  Finally, $\{0x91\} \bullet \{0x37\} = \{0xB4\}$

22 .2.2 Byte Substitution Box (S-box) Generation

Byte substitution is a non-linear transformation of bytes. The input byte (8 bits) is used as the index to the S-box to get the substituting byte out. Byte substitution is used in the key expansion and in the round processing.

22 .2.2.1 The Mathematical Matrix Computation

The S-box is created in two transformations:

1. Find the multiplicative inverse in the finite field of the index (8 bits) to the S-box, except the {00} index which is mapped to itself. The computation in finite field is different from the number computation. For example, the multiplicative inverse of {0xC6} is {0xE4}.

   {0xC6} = {1 1 0 0 0 1 1 0}
   {0xE4} = {1 1 1 0 0 1 0 0}
   {1 1 0 0 0 1 1 0} ● {1 1 1 0 0 1 0 0}
   = {1 0 0 1 0 0 1 0 1 0 1 1 0 0 0}/
     {1 0 0 0 1 1 0 1 1}
   = {1 0 0 1 1 1 1}, and the remainder: 1

2. Apply the affine transformation to the multiplicate inverse. The affine transformation consists of a multiplication with a matrix then followed by a vector addition.

$$
\begin{bmatrix} b'_0 \\ b'_1 \\ b'_2 \\ b'_3 \\ b'_4 \\ b'_5 \\ b'_6 \\ b'_7 \end{bmatrix} = \begin{bmatrix} 1&0&0&0&1&1&1&1 \\ 1&1&0&0&0&1&1&1 \\ 1&1&1&0&0&0&1&1 \\ 1&1&1&1&0&0&0&1 \\ 1&1&1&1&1&0&0&0 \\ 0&1&1&1&1&1&0&0 \\ 0&0&1&1&1&1&1&0 \\ 0&0&0&1&1&1&1&1 \end{bmatrix} \begin{bmatrix} b_0 \\ b_1 \\ b_2 \\ b_3 \\ b_4 \\ b_5 \\ b_6 \\ b_7 \end{bmatrix} + \begin{bmatrix} 1 \\ 1 \\ 0 \\ 0 \\ 0 \\ 1 \\ 1 \\ 0 \end{bmatrix}
$$

Figure 51: Affine Transformation

Now the affine transformation is performed in two steps. The multiplicative inverse of {0xC6} is {0xE4}. Put the bit pattern of {0xE4} in the vector. Remember the least significant bit is placed on the top of the vector. The result of matrix multiplication is {0xD7} (see the following figure):

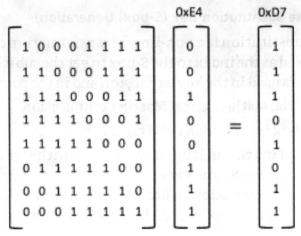

Figure 52: Matrix Multiplication

Then the result {0xD7} is added (XOR) with {0x63} which is the substitution byte of zero. Finally, the substitution byte of {0xC6} is {0xB4}:

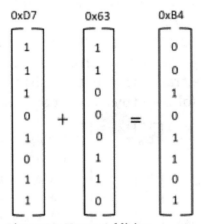

Figure 53: Vector Addition

22 .2.2.2 Software Implementation

It is difficult to find the multiplicative inverse by matrix computation. Fortunately, the Extended Euclidean Algorithm mentioned in section 21.3.2 works fine for finding the multiplicative inverse in finite field. Through Extended Euclidean Algorithm, the multiplicative inverse of {0xC6} is {0xE4}.

The concept in the mathematical matrix form is for the human to understand the affine transformation. Another way is to use the software to compute the affine transformation at the bit-level:

$b'_i = b_i \oplus b_{(i+4) \bmod 8} \oplus b_{(i+5) \bmod 8} \oplus b_{(i+6) \bmod 8} \oplus b_{(i+7) \bmod 8} \oplus C_i$
    where $0 <= i < 8$,
    b_0 is the least significant bit,
    b_i is the ith bit of the byte,
    C_i is the ith bit of $\{0x63\} = \{01100011\}$,
    b' is the updated bit.

The bit-level transformation can be expanded as follows:
$b'_7 = b_7 \oplus b_3 \oplus b_4 \oplus b_5 \oplus b_6 \oplus C_7$
$b'_6 = b_6 \oplus b_2 \oplus b_3 \oplus b_4 \oplus b_5 \oplus C_6$
$b'_5 = b_5 \oplus b_1 \oplus b_2 \oplus b_3 \oplus b_4 \oplus C_5$
$b'_4 = b_4 \oplus b_0 \oplus b_1 \oplus b_2 \oplus b_3 \oplus C_4$
$b'_3 = b_3 \oplus b_7 \oplus b_0 \oplus b_1 \oplus b_2 \oplus C_3$
$b'_2 = b_2 \oplus b_6 \oplus b_7 \oplus b_0 \oplus b_1 \oplus C_2$
$b'_1 = b_1 \oplus b_5 \oplus b_6 \oplus b_7 \oplus b_0 \oplus C_1$
$b'_0 = b_0 \oplus b_4 \oplus b_5 \oplus b_6 \oplus b_7 \oplus C_0$

The above bit-bit level transformation can be further summarized to the byte-level transformation:

$y = x \oplus \textbf{ROTLF}(x, 4) \oplus \textbf{ROTLF}(x, 3) \oplus \textbf{ROTLF}(x, 2) \oplus \textbf{ROTLF}(x, 1) \oplus C$
    where x is the input byte,
    y is the output byte,
    ROTLF(x, n) is the macro for circularly rotating x left by n bits,
    $C = \{0x63\} = \{01100011\}$.

Here is the relation between the bit-level and the byte-level:
Let $x = \{b_7 b_6 b_5 b_4 b_3 b_2 b_1 b_0\}$. The bit order of x matches the 1st column in the bit-level transformation.

After x is circularly rotated to the left
- by 4 bits, the result is $\{b_3 b_2 b_1 b_0 b_7 b_6 b_5 b_4\}$, i.e. ROTLF(x, 4) in byte-level or the 2nd column in the expanded bit-level.
- by 3 bits, the result is $\{b_4 b_3 b_2 b_1 b_0 b_7 b_6 b_5\}$, i.e. ROTLF(x, 3) in byte-level or the 3rd column in the expanded bit-level.
- by 2 bits, the result is $\{b_5 b_4 b_3 b_2 b_1 b_0 b_7 b_6\}$, i.e. ROTLF(x,

2) in byte-level or the 4th column in the expanded bit-level.

- by 1 bits, the result is { b_6 b_5 b_4 b_3 b_2 b_1 b_0 b_7 }, i.e. ROTLF(x, 1) in byte-level or the 5th column in the expanded bit-level.

So, the byte-level affine transformation matches the bit-level affine transformation.

Therefore, the byte-level affine transformation can be implemented in C/C++ code:

Let x = 0xE4

0xB4 = x ^ ROTLF(x, 4) ^ ROTLF(x, 3) ^ ROTLF(x, 2) ^ ROTLF(x, 1) ^ 0x63
    where ROTLF(x, n) = ((uint_8) (x << n) | (x >> (8 - n)))

22.2.2.3 Forward S-Box Table

The above processes generate the following S-Box:

Least significant nibble of the byte

	00	01	02	03	04	05	06	07	08	09	0a	0b	0c	0d	0e	0f
00	63	7c	77	7b	f2	6b	6f	c5	30	01	67	2b	fe	d7	ab	76
10	ca	82	c9	7d	fa	59	47	f0	ad	d4	a2	af	9c	a4	72	c0
20	b7	fd	93	26	36	3f	f7	cc	34	a5	e5	f1	71	d8	31	15
30	04	c7	23	c3	18	96	05	9a	07	12	80	e2	eb	27	b2	75
40	09	83	2c	1a	1b	6e	5a	a0	52	3b	d6	b3	29	e3	2f	84
50	53	d1	00	ed	20	fc	b1	5b	6a	cb	be	39	4a	4c	58	cf
60	d0	ef	aa	fb	43	4d	33	85	45	f9	02	7f	50	3c	9f	a8
70	51	a3	40	8f	92	9d	38	f5	bc	b6	da	21	10	ff	f3	d2
80	cd	0c	13	ec	5f	97	44	17	c4	a7	7e	3d	64	5d	19	73
90	60	81	4f	dc	22	2a	90	88	46	ee	b8	14	de	5e	0b	db
a0	e0	32	3a	0a	49	06	24	5c	c2	d3	ac	62	91	95	e4	79
b0	e7	c8	37	6d	8d	d5	4e	a9	6c	56	f4	ea	65	7a	ae	08
c0	ba	78	25	2e	1c	a6	b4	c6	e8	dd	74	1f	4b	bd	8b	8a
d0	70	3e	b5	66	48	03	f6	0e	61	35	57	b9	86	c1	1d	9e
e0	e1	f8	98	11	69	d9	8e	94	9b	1e	87	e9	ce	55	28	df
f0	8c	a1	89	0d	bf	e6	42	68	41	99	2d	0f	b0	54	bb	16

Most significant nibble of the byte

Figure 54: Forward (Encryption) Byte Substitution Box

The pseudo code for generating the forward S-Box and inverse S-Box is as follows:

```
#define ROTLF(x,shift) ((uint8_t) (x << shift) | (x >> (8 - shift)))
void GenerateSBoxes(uint8_t fwdsbox[256])
{
    /* 0 is a special case since it has no inverse */
    fwdsbox[0] = 0x63;

    mod = 0x11B; // X^8 + X^4 + X^3 + X + 1 = (100011011)
    indx = 1;
    while (indx < 256)
    {
        // Use Extended Euclidean Algorithm to find the multiplicative inverse
        b = GF_xgcd(indx, mod);

        // Compute the affine transformation
        affx = b ^ ROTLF(b, 4) ^ ROTLF(b, 3) ^ ROTLF(b, 2) ^ ROTLF(b, 1);

        temp = affx ^ 0x63;
        fwdsbox[indx] = temp;   // Forward S-Box

        invsbox[temp] = indx;   // Inverse S-Box

        ++indx;
    }
}
```

Figure 55: Pseudo code for Generating Forward S-Box

22 .2.3 Inverse (Decryption) Byte Substitution Box Generation

The inverse byte substitution box is the opposite of the byte substitution box. The easiest way to generate the inverse S-Box is to swap the index and the substituted byte while generating the forward S-Box, i.e., use the substituted byte as the index to the inverse S-Box, and the contents is the original index. In the above forward pseudo code, the inverse S-Box is "invsbox[temp] = indx;" after "fwdsbox[indx] = temp;" (see the above figure).

The inverse S-Box also can be calculated by the inverse of affine transformation, then followed by the multiplicative inverse in the finite field:

- First, calculate the affine transformation which can be obtained by the following bit-level transformation:

$$b'_i = b_{(i+2) \bmod 8} \oplus b_{(i+5) \bmod 8} \oplus b_{(i+7) \bmod 8} \oplus D_i$$

where $0 <= i < 8$,

$D = 0x05 = \{0\,0\,0\,0\,0\,1\,0\,1\}$,

b_0 is the least significant bit.

The bit-level transformation can be expanded as follows:

$b'_7 = b_1 \oplus b_4 \oplus b_6 \oplus D_7$
$b'_6 = b_0 \oplus b_3 \oplus b_5 \oplus D_6$
$b'_5 = b_7 \oplus b_2 \oplus b_4 \oplus D_5$
$b'_4 = b_6 \oplus b_1 \oplus b_3 \oplus D_4$
$b'_3 = b_5 \oplus b_0 \oplus b_2 \oplus D_3$
$b'_2 = b_4 \oplus b_7 \oplus b_1 \oplus D_2$
$b'_1 = b_3 \oplus b_6 \oplus b_0 \oplus D_1$
$b'_0 = b_2 \oplus b_5 \oplus b_7 \oplus D_0$

The above bit-bit level affine transformation can be summarized into the byte-level affine transformation:

$$x = ROTLF(y, 1) \oplus ROTLF(y, 3) \oplus ROTLF(y, 6) \oplus D$$

Let $y = \{b_7\ b_6\ b_5\ b_4\ b_3\ b_2\ b_1\ b_0\}$. After y is circularly shifted to the left

- by 1 bits, the result is $\{b_6\ b_5\ b_4\ b_3\ b_2\ b_1\ b_0\ b_7\}$, i.e. $ROTLF(y, 1)$

EMBEDDED SYSTEM ENGINEERING GUIDE

in byte-level or the 3rd column in the expanded bit-level.

- by 3 bits, the result is $\{b_4\ b_3\ b_2\ b_1\ b_0\ b_7\ b_6\ b_5\}$, i.e. ROTLF(y, 3) in or byte-level the 2nd column in the expanded bit-level.
- by 6 bits, the result is $\{b_1\ b_0\ b_7\ b_6\ b_5\ b_4\ b_3\ b_2\}$, i.e. ROTLF(y, 6) in byte-level or the 1st column in the expanded bit-level.

So, the byte-level affine transformation matches the bit-level affine transformation.

- After the affine transformation, then find the multiplicative inverse in finite field by the Extended Euclidean Algorithm. The result is the inverse substituted byte.

Least significant nibble of the byte

	00	01	02	03	04	05	06	07	08	09	0a	0b	0c	0d	0e	0f
00	52	09	6a	d5	30	36	a5	38	bf	40	a3	9e	81	f3	d7	fb
10	7c	e3	39	82	9b	2f	ff	87	34	8e	43	44	c4	de	e9	cb
20	54	7b	94	32	a6	c2	23	3d	ee	4c	95	0b	42	fa	c3	4e
30	08	2e	a1	66	28	d9	24	b2	76	5b	a2	49	6d	8b	d1	25
40	72	f8	f6	64	86	68	98	16	d4	a4	5c	cc	5d	65	b6	92
50	6c	70	48	50	fd	ed	b9	da	5e	15	46	57	a7	8d	9d	84
60	90	d8	ab	00	8c	bc	d3	0a	f7	e4	58	05	b8	b3	45	06
70	d0	2c	1e	8f	ca	3f	0f	02	c1	af	bd	03	01	13	8a	6b
80	3a	91	11	41	4f	67	dc	ea	97	f2	cf	ce	f0	b4	e6	73
90	96	ac	74	22	e7	ad	35	85	e2	f9	37	e8	1c	75	df	6e
a0	47	f1	1a	71	1d	29	c5	89	6f	b7	62	0e	aa	18	be	1b
b0	fc	56	3e	4b	c6	d2	79	20	9a	db	c0	fe	78	cd	5a	f4
c0	1f	dd	a8	33	88	07	c7	31	b1	12	10	59	27	80	ec	5f
d0	60	51	7f	a9	19	b5	4a	0d	2d	e5	7a	9f	93	c9	9c	ef
e0	a0	e0	3b	4d	ae	2a	f5	b0	c8	eb	bb	3c	83	53	99	61
f0	17	2b	04	7e	ba	77	d6	26	e1	69	14	63	55	21	0c	7d

Figure 56: Inverse (Decryption) Byte Substitution Box

22 .2.4 Key Expansion

Each round has its own round key words which are expanded from the Cypher Key. The purpose of the key expansion is to reduce the predictivity of the key. It makes the key difficult for the hacker to find the pattern.

The length of the Cypher Key can be 128 bits, 192 bits, or 256 bits. The following steps take the Cypher Key, and perform Key Expansion to generate the round key schedule. The length of the round key schedule is (Nb x (Nr + 1)), where Nb and Nr are defined in Figure 49: Summary of Key, Block and Round. Each round key word is 32 bits.

- In the current standard, the length of the cipher message is limited to 128 bits. So, Nb is fixed to 4 (128/32).
- Combine the cypher keys from bytes to words. The first 4 bytes of the Cypher Key construct the first word, W_0. The next 4 bytes forms word W_1, and so on. See the following figure:

Figure 57: Cypher Keys from Bytes to Words

- Please note that the first byte of the Cypher Key is placed at the most significant byte (MSB) of the word, W_0, i.e., bit 31-24 for little endian. The second byte is placed at bit 23-16, The third byte is at bit 15-8, and the fourth byte is at 7-0. The same principles are applied to the rest of the words.
- This creates the first 4 (128 / 32) words of round key words for 128-bit Cypher Key, the first 6 (192 / 32) round key words for 192-bit Cypher Key, and the first 8 (256 / 32) round key words for 256-bit Cypher Key. These first key words will be used to generate the rest of the key words.
- For the 128-bit Cypher Key, there are 10 rounds of transformation, plus a pre-round transformation. Each round will need 4 key words. So, the total round key schedule (including the pre-round trans-

formation) for 128-bit Cypher Key is 44 (4 x 11) key words. From the first 4 key words, another 40 key words will be generated.

- For the 192-bit Cypher Key, there are 12 rounds of transformation, plus a pre-round transformation. So, the length of the round key schedule is 52 (4 x 13) key words. From the first 6 key words, another 46 key words will be generated.
- For the 256-bit Cypher Key, there are 14 rounds of transformation, plus a pre-round transformation, So, the length of the round key schedule is 60 (4 x 15) key words. From the first 8 key words, another 52 key words will be generated.

Here is the example of how to generate the rest of the 40 words for 128-bit Cypher Key. Each round has 4 key words. The first round (pre-round) group has 4 key word, W_0, W_1, W_2, W_3 from the 128-bit cypher key.

To compute the next group of 4 words for round 1:

$W_4 = W_0 \oplus ((\text{SubByte}(\text{RotateWord}(W_3))) \oplus \text{Rcon}[1])$

$W_5 = W_4 \oplus W_1$

$W_6 = W_5 \oplus W_2$

$W_7 = W_6 \oplus W_3$

And the next 4 words for round 2:

$W_8 = W_4 \oplus ((\text{SubByte}(\text{RotateWord}(W_7))) \oplus \text{Rcon}[2])$

$W_9 = W_8 \oplus W_5$

$W_{10} = W_9 \oplus W_6$

$W_{11} = W_{10} \oplus W_7$

The computation can be summarized as follows:

$W_{i+4} = W_{i+0} \oplus ((\text{SubByte}(\text{RotateWord}(W_{i+3}))) \oplus \text{Rcon}[k])$

$W_{i+5} = W_{i+4} \oplus W_{i+1}$

$W_{i+6} = W_{i+5} \oplus W_{i+2}$

$W_{i+7} = W_{i+6} \oplus W_{i+3}$

where i is the starting word of each group, i.e., i = (round – 1) * 4.
k is the round number.

The RotateWord, SubByte, and Rcon functions are defined as follows:

- Rotate Word (RotateWord) – The 32-bit key word is rotated to the left by 1 byte (8 bits).

- Byte Substitution (SubByte) – After the key word is rotated, each byte in the word is substituted by using the forward S-Box (see section 22.3.2).
- Round Constant (Rcon) – The 3 least-significant-byte of the Round Constant word is zero, i.e., Rcon[k] = {RC[k], 0x00, 0x00, 0x00}, where k is the round number, and RC[k] is obtained by the following rules:

  RC[1] = 0x01
  RC[k] = RC[k – 1] << 1

  So, RC[1] = 0x01, RC[2] = 0x02, RC[3] = 0x04, RC[4] = 0x08, ... etc.
  when RC[k] > 0x80, RC[k] = RC[k] ⊕ 0x11B
  where 0x11B = {1 0 0 0 1 1 0 1 1} = $X^8 + X^4 + X^3 + X + 1$

Here is the pseudo code for the key expanding of the round key schedule (including the pre-round keys):

```
KeyExpansion(uint8_t Key[], uint32_t word[Nb * (Nr + 1)], Nk)
{
    i = 0;
    while (i < Nk)
    {
        word[i] = WORD(Key[4*i], Key[4*i+1], Key[4*i+2], Key[4*i+3]);
        ++i;
    }

    i = Nk;
    rcon = 0x01;
    while (i < (Nb * (Nr + 1)))
    {
        temp = word[i – 1];
        if ((i mod Nk) == 0)
        {
            temp = RotWord(temp);
            temp = SubWord(temp);
            temp = temp XOR (rcon << 24);

            rcon = rcon << 1;
            if (rcon > 0x80)
            {
                rcon = rcon XOR 0x11B;
            }   // if
        }   // if
        else
        {
            If ((Nk > 6) && ((i mod Nk) == 4)
            {
                temp = SubWord(temp);
            }
        }   // else
        word[i] = word[i – Nk] XOR temp;
        ++i;
    }   // while
}
```

Figure 58 : Key Expansion

22 .3 Encryption

Before performing the round transformation, the 128-bit message (16 bytes) is copied into a 4 x 4 state array (see section 22.1). After that, the pre-round transformation (AddRoundKey) adds the pre-round key words to the state array. Then followed by the round loop transformations. In each round, SubBytes, ShiftRows, MixColumns, and AddRoundKey transformations are performed, except the last round in which only SubBytes, ShiftRows, and AddRoundKey transformations are processed, and MixColumns transformation is excluded from the last round.

Here is the pseudo code for encryption:

```
Encryption (uint8_t in[], uint8_t out[], uint32_t roundKey[])
{
     uint8_t State[4][Nb];

     i = 0;
     for (collndx = 0; collndx < Nb; ++collndx)
     {
          for (rowIndx = 0; rowIndx < 4; ++rowIndx)
          {
               State[rowIndx][collndx] = in[i];
               ++i;
          }
     }

     AddRoundKey(State, *roundKey[0]);
     for (round = 1; round < Nr; ++ round)
     {
          SubBytes(State);
          ShiftRows(State);
          MixColumns(State);
          AddRoundKey(State, *roundKey[round * Nb]);
     }

     SubBytes(State);
     ShiftRows(State);
     AddRoundKey(State, *roundKey[Nr * Nb]);

     i = 0;
     for (collndx = 0; collndx < Nb; ++collndx)
     {
          for (rowIndx = 0; rowIndx < 4; ++rowIndx)
          {
               out[i] = State[rowIndx][collndx];
               ++i;
          }
     }
}
```

Figure 59: Pseudo Code of Encryption

22 .3.1 AddRoundKey Transformation

The State Array in the round loop has Nb (in this standard, Nb is fixed at 4) columns, and each column has 4 bytes. A Round Key contains a set of Nb (4) words. In this transformation, a Round Key is added (bitwise XORed) to the State Array. Each word is 4 bytes which are applied to a column of the State Array. The Nb round words are coming from the round key schedule which is expanded in section 22.2.4. In a round, the first word of Round Key is from the offset of (round * Nb) words in the round key schedule (see Figure 60: State Array vs Round Key). The most significant byte (MSB) of the word is XORed with the top byte (S_0,**c**) of the column. The second byte of the word is XORed with the second byte (S_1,**c**) of the column, and so on.

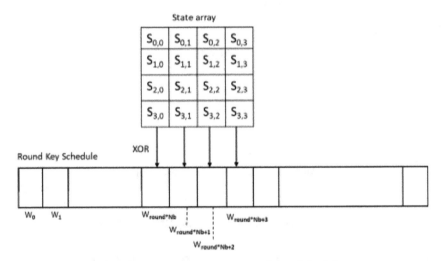

Figure 60: State Array vs Round Key Schedule

For example, column 1 of the State Array is XORed with the Round Key word:

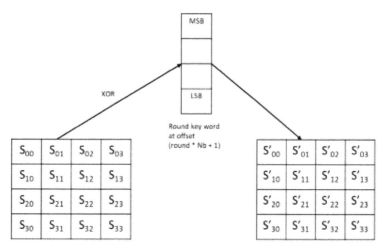

Figure 61: Column 1 of State Array Is XORed with Round Key Word

22 .3.2 SubBytes Transformation

This transformation is non-linear byte substitution. Each byte in the State array is substituted with the corresponding byte in the forward S-Box.

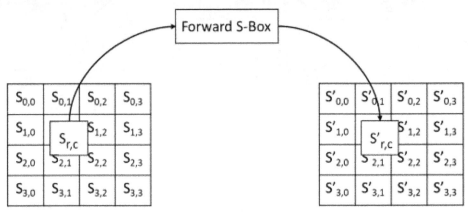

Figure 62: Byte Substitution

There are two different approaches to access the S-box.

1. If the S-Box is a 2-dimensional table, the input 8 bits is split into 2 nibbles (4 bits each). The most significant nibble is used as the row index, and the least significant nibble is used as the column index to the table. Then the substituted byte is extracted from the table. From the example in Section 22.2.2, to get the substituted byte of {0xC6}, the indices are 0xC for the row, and 0x6 for the column. The substituted byte of {0xC6} from Figure 54: Forward (Encryption) Byte Substitution Box is {0xB4}.

2. Since a byte represents a number from 0 to 255 (0xFF), the 2-dimensional table can be flattened to 1-dimensional array of 256 bytes. The substituted byte is then extracted from the 1-dimensional array. From the example in Section 22.2.2, {0xC6} is used as the index to the 1-dimensional S-Box, and {0xB4} is extracted.

22 .3.3 ShiftRows Transformation

In order to scramble the byte order in the 128-bit message, the bytes in rows of the State array are circularly shifted to the left, except the first row. For those bytes that are shifted out the row are appended at the end of the row. Here is how the ShiftRows works:

- The bytes in the first row of the State array are not shifted. They stay in the same order.
- On the second row, one byte is circularly shifted to the left. Byte $S_{1,0}$ is shifted out and appended at the end of the row. Byte $S_{1,1}$ is shifted to the left, and becomes the leading byte of the second row.
- On the third row, two bytes are shifted to the left. Byte $S_{2,0}$ and byte $S_{2,1}$ are shifted out and appended at the end of the row. Byte $S_{2,2}$ becomes the leading byte of the third row.
- On the fourth row, three bytes are shifted to the left. Byte $S_{3,0}$, Byte $S_{3,1}$ and byte $S_{3,2}$ are shifted out, and appended at the end of the row. Byte $S_{3,3}$ becomes the leading byte of the fourth row.

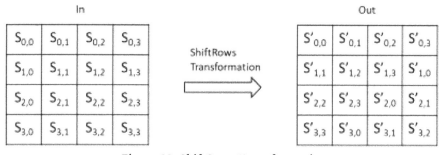

Figure 63: ShiftRows Transformation

22 .3.4 MixColumns Transformation

More scrambling to the 128-bit message, each column of the State Array multiplies with a 4 x 4 fixed matrix.

$$
\begin{bmatrix}
02 & 03 & 01 & 01 \\
01 & 02 & 03 & 01 \\
01 & 01 & 02 & 03 \\
03 & 01 & 01 & 02
\end{bmatrix}
\begin{bmatrix}
S_{0,c} \\
S_{1,c} \\
S_{2,c} \\
S_{3,c}
\end{bmatrix}
=
\begin{bmatrix}
S'_{0,c} \\
S'_{1,c} \\
S'_{2,c} \\
S'_{3,c}
\end{bmatrix}
$$

Figure 64: The Fixed Matrix Multiply with a Column

Please note that the multiplication and addition are performed in Finite Field. This matrix multiplication can be expanded as the followings:

$$S'_{0,c} = (\{02\} \bullet S_{0,c}) \oplus (\{03\} \bullet S_{1,c}) \oplus (\{01\} \bullet S_{2,c}) \oplus (\{01\} \bullet S_{3,c})$$
$$S'_{1,c} = (\{01\} \bullet S_{0,c}) \oplus (\{02\} \bullet S_{1,c}) \oplus (\{03\} \bullet S_{2,c}) \oplus (\{01\} \bullet S_{3,c})$$
$$S'_{2,c} = (\{01\} \bullet S_{0,c}) \oplus (\{01\} \bullet S_{1,c}) \oplus (\{02\} \bullet S_{2,c}) \oplus (\{03\} \bullet S_{3,c})$$
$$S'_{3,c} = (\{03\} \bullet S_{0,c}) \oplus (\{01\} \bullet S_{1,c}) \oplus (\{01\} \bullet S_{2,c}) \oplus (\{02\} \bullet S_{3,c})$$

Since $(\{01\} \bullet S_{r,c}) = S_{r,c}$, the above equations can be simplified as follows:

$$S'_{0,c} = (\{02\} \bullet S_{0,c}) \oplus (\{03\} \bullet S_{1,c}) \oplus S_{2,c} \oplus S_{3,c}$$
$$S'_{1,c} = S_{0,c} \oplus (\{02\} \bullet S_{1,c}) \oplus (\{03\} \bullet S_{2,c}) \oplus S_{3,c}$$
$$S'_{2,c} = S_{0,c} \oplus S_{1,c} \oplus (\{02\} \bullet S_{2,c}) \oplus (\{03\} \bullet S_{3,c})$$
$$S'_{3,c} = (\{03\} \bullet S_{0,c}) \oplus S_{1,c} \oplus S_{2,c} \oplus (\{02\} \bullet S_{3,c})$$

The result of the multiplication and XORing is placed in the corresponding column in the output array.

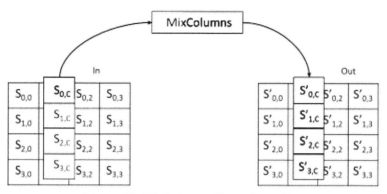

Figure 65 : MixColumns Transformation

22 .4 Decryption

The process of decryption is basically the inverse of the encryption. The transformation routines used in each round are InvShiftRows, InvSubBytes, AddRoundKey, and InvMixColumns as shown in the following pseudo code. Similar to the encryption, the pre-round process performs only AddRoundKey transformation. In each round, InvShiftRows, InvSubBytes, AddRoundKey, and InvMixColumns transformations are processed, except the last round which only InvShiftRows, InvSubBytes, and AddRoundKey transformations are processed. The last round doesn't include InvMixColumns transformation.

Here is the pseudo code for decryption:

```
Decryption (uint8_t in[], uint8_t out[], uint32_t roundKey[])
{
    uint8_t State[4][Nb];

    i = 0;
    for (colIndx = 0; colIndx < Nb; ++colIndx)
    {
        for (rowIndx = 0; rowIndx < 4; ++rowIndx)
        {
            // Move ciphered message to State array
            State[rowIndx][colIndx] = in[i];
            ++i;
        }
    }

    AddRoundKey(State, *roundKey[Nr * Nb]);
    for (round = (Nr − 1); round > 0; --round)
    {
        InvShiftRows(State);
        InvSubBytes(State);
        AddRoundKey(State, *roundKey[round * Nb]);
        InvMixColumns(State);
    }

    InvShiftRows(State);
    InvSubBytes(State);
    AddRoundKey(State, *roundKey[0]);

    i = 0;
    for (colIndx = 0; colIndx < Nb; ++colIndx)
    {
        for (rowIndx = 0; rowIndx < 4; ++rowIndx)
        {
            out[i] = State[rowIndx][colIndx];
            ++i;
        }
    }
}
```

Figure 66: Pseudo Code for Decryption

22 .4.1 InvShiftRows Transformation

As opposite to the encryption, the rows are shifted to the right. Here is how the InvShiftRows is performed:

- The bytes in the first row of the State Array are not shifted. They stay in the same order.
- On the second row, one byte is circularly shifted to the right. Byte $S_{1,3}$ is shifted out and added to the beginning of the row. The rest bytes are shifted to the right by one position. Byte $S_{1,2}$ becomes the end of the second row.
- On the third row, two bytes are shifted to the right. Byte $S_{2,2}$ and byte $S_{2,3}$ are shifted out and added to the beginning of the row. Byte $S_{2,2}$ becomes the leading byte of the third row. Byte $S_{2,1}$ becomes the end byte.
- On the fourth row, three bytes are shifted to the right. Byte $S_{3,1}$, Byte $S_{3,2}$ and byte $S_{3,3}$ are shifted out, and added to the beginning of the row. Byte $S_{3,1}$ becomes the leading byte of the fourth row. Byte $S_{3,0}$ becomes the last byte of the fourth row.

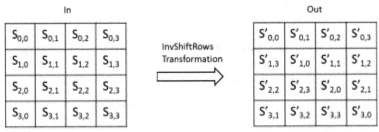

Figure 67: InvShiftRows Transformation

22.4.2 InvSubBytes Transformation

This transformation is the inverse of the byte substitution transformation. It is the same as SubBytes Transformation in section 22.3.2. The only difference is that this transformation applies the inverse S-Box, instead of the forward S-Box.

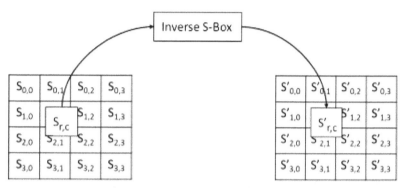

Figure 68 : Inverse Byte Substitution

22 .4.3 InvMixColumns Transformation

This transformation is the inverse of MixColumns transformation (see section 22.3.4). Here the 4 x 4 fixed matrix is different.

$$
\begin{bmatrix}
0e & 0b & 0d & 09 \\
09 & 0e & 0b & 0d \\
0d & 09 & 0e & 0b \\
0b & 0d & 09 & 0e
\end{bmatrix}
\begin{bmatrix}
S_{0,c} \\
S_{1,c} \\
S_{2,c} \\
S_{3,c}
\end{bmatrix}
=
\begin{bmatrix}
S'_{0,c} \\
S'_{1,c} \\
S'_{2,c} \\
S'_{3,c}
\end{bmatrix}
$$

Figure 69: Inverse Fixed Polynomial for Column Multiplication

Matrix multiplication and addition can be expanded to the following:

$S'_{0,c} = (\{0e\} \bullet S_{0,c}) \oplus (\{0b\} \bullet S_{1,c}) \oplus (\{0d\} \bullet S_{2,c}) \oplus (\{09\} \bullet S_{3,c})$
$S'_{1,c} = (\{09\} \bullet S_{0,c}) \oplus (\{0e\} \bullet S_{1,c}) \oplus (\{0b\} \bullet S_{2,c}) \oplus (\{0d\} \bullet S_{3,c})$
$S'_{2,c} = (\{0d\} \bullet S_{0,c}) \oplus (\{09\} \bullet S_{1,c}) \oplus (\{0e\} \bullet S_{2,c}) \oplus (\{0b\} \bullet S_{3,c})$
$S'_{3,c} = (\{0b\} \bullet S_{0,c}) \oplus (\{0d\} \bullet S_{1,c}) \oplus (\{09\} \bullet S_{2,c}) \oplus (\{0e\} \bullet S_{3,c})$

The result of the multiplication and XORing of a column is placed in the corresponding column of the output array.

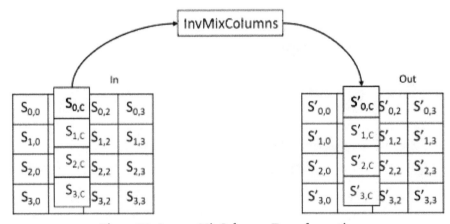

Figure 70: Inverse MixColumns Transformation

23 Future of the Embedded System

Human being's demand is the motivation of innovations and inventions. To meet the human needs, the industry will come up new solutions. As the human demand increases and the technology also advances, the future of the embedded system is unlimited.

According to ARM Inc's prediction, by the year 2035 there will be a trillion devices in every corner of the world. IoT will become the mainstream of the embedded industry. How to handle so many devices is becoming an issue. And how to keep the device secured is even more important. Here are some thoughts that will impact the embedded system in the future.

23 .1 Speed and Size

The technology will make the future products more sophisticated. The present products become smaller, faster and have more functions. Reducing the size of the IC die also can save energy.

23.2 Security

Besides speed and size, security is another important subject, especially in IoT industry. There are hackers out there to attack the systems. To protect the intellectual property and the integrity of the product, security is a must for now and in the future. In addition to Secure Boot and Root of Trust, more hardware and software supports are needed to keep the IoT device secured.

23 .3 Connectivity

For IoT products, what kind of connectivity to use is a big decision. When choosing connectivity, it is necessary to consider the power consumption, transmit/receive distance, and data bandwidth. The ideal connectivity is the low power consumption, long range transmission, and large data bandwidth. But it is hard to achieve the ideality. Depending on where IoT devices are deployed, it requires different method of connectivity. If IoT devices are installed in the building, such empty parking lots indicators in the parking garage, WIFI, Bluetooth or Ethernet can do the job. But if IoT devices are installed in the mountains to monitor the earthquake or the weather, they need cellular or satellite connectivity.

Another concern for connectivity is the cost. Although cellular or satellite connectivity is more flexible, they cost more. 5G cellular network provides service to more devices in a square mile. It will benefit IoT in the future. But again, the cost is still uncertain.

To make the connectivity more efficient is to make IoT device smarter on the edge, and reduce the traffic between the device and the cloud. During RF transmitting and receiving, the power consumption is much higher than the local processing. So, IoT edge device can make its own decision through Artificial Intelligence/Machine Learning, instead sending a bunch of data to the cloud and waiting for the result.

23 .4 Battery Life

Many IoT devices are deployed in the remote area or carried by a person, such as humidity sensors in the farmland or digital cameras, digital watches. They are unable to use the plug-in electricity. Power consumption is always a concern during the design. How to preserve the battery consumption is big challenge. Increasing the battery size can help, but it is not practical solution because it is heavy to carry.

For some devices, solar panel is a good solution. In the daytime, the panel can generate power. The device can use the generated power, and save the surplus power to the battery. So, in the evening, the device can use the saved power.

How to prolong the battery life is a big challenge. Not only new technology is needed, but also needs to improve the efficiency. Battery life is greatly influenced by software which can control the device low power mode (hibernation) and the duration of transmission. To conserve power, the device can be kept in sleep mode, and wake up only when there is an activity.

23 .5 Artificial Intelligence (AI) and Machine Learning (ML)

Machine Learning is a subset of AI. It teaches the computer to learn from the input data. One approach for the machine learning is to feed the computer repeatedly with the images of an object. The computer stores the training images in the database. So, when the same object is shown to the machine, the machine can recognize the object. But when a different object is shown, the machine might get it wrong.

Another approach for AI is using "inference" which is more human like. It makes the decision by reasoning. For example, when the sky is full of low dark clouds, the machine predicts that it is going to rain. Inference is making logical conclusion by the experience or by the known facts. Another example, when an animal hides behand a bush. Only the tail can be seen. Depending on the shape of the tail, the machine can guess what kind of animal it might be. Like human beings, sometimes this approach might get the wrong prediction, too. But this approach is much closer to human being's reasoning.

23 .6 Post-Quantum Cryptography

Although it is pretty hard to crack the code of the RSA Public-key Cryptosystem and Advanced Encryption Standard (AES), the recent invention of quantum computers which have much more computation power than the traditional bits computers. It is becoming a threat to the cryptographic systems. New methods or new approaches to the cryptography are needed to withstand the future quantum attacks from the hackers.

References

[1] Knuth Donald E. "<u>The Art of Computer Programming</u>", Vol 2, Addison-Wesley Publishing Co., Reading, Massachusetts, 1981.

[2] "<u>The Advanced Encryption Standard</u>", FIPS PUB 197: the official AES standard. Federal Information Processing Standard. 2001-11-26. Retrieved 2010-04-29

[3] "MPC8280 PowerQUICC™ II Family Reference Manual", Rev. 1, 12/2005, Freescale Semiconductor, Chandler, Arizona

Appendix

Here is the sample C code for CRC computation, RSA Public Key Cryptosystem and Advanced Encryption Standard. Although the code has been tested on Microsoft Visual Studio 2019, it is for reference only. Microsoft Visual Studio 2019 is a free download for individuals. For details about the download, please check at the Microsoft website.

A. Cyclic Redundancy Check

Compute CRC32 On-The-Fly:

```c
uint32_t computeCrcOnTheFly(
    uint8_t message[],
    uint32_t msgLen)
{
    uint32_t lenIndx, bitIndx;
    uint32_t crc32;
    uint32_t byte;

    // Compute CRC32 bit by bit
    crc32 = 0xffffffff;
    for (lenIndx = 0; lenIndx < msgLen; ++lenIndx)
    {
        byte = message[lenIndx];
        crc32 = crc32 ^ byte;
        for (bitIndx = 0; bitIndx < 8; ++bitIndx)
        {
            if (crc32 & 0x01)
            {
                crc32 = (crc32 >> 1) ^ 0xEDB88320;
            }
            else
            {
                crc32 = crc32 >> 1;
            }
        }
    }
    crc32 = ~crc32;

    return crc32;
}
```

Compute the CRC32 with the table driven:

```
uint32_t crc32Table[256];

// First, build the CRC table
buildCRC32Table(crc32Table);

uint32_t tableDrivenCrc(
uint8_t message[],
uint32_t msgLen)
{
    uint32_t lenIndx;      // indx,
    uint32_t tabCrc32;
    uint32_t byte;
    uint32_t tabIndx;

    // Table-driven CRC32
    tabCrc32 = 0xFFFFFFFF;
    for (lenIndx = 0; lenIndx < msgLen; ++lenIndx)
    {
        byte = message[lenIndx];
        tabIndx = (byte ^ tabCrc32) & 0xFF;
        tabCrc32 = (tabCrc32 >> 8) ^ crc32Table[tabIndx];
    }
    tabCrc32 = ~tabCrc32;

    return tabCrc32;
}

// Build CRC32 table
void buildCRC32Table(uint32_t crcTable[])
{
    uint32_t tabIndx, bitIndx;
    uint32_t crc32 = 0;

    for (tabIndx = 0; tabIndx < 256; ++tabIndx)
    {
        crc32 = tabIndx;
        for (bitIndx = 0; bitIndx < 8; ++bitIndx)
        {
            if (crc32 & 0x01)
            {
                crc32 = (crc32 >> 1) ^ 0xEDB88320;
            }
            else
            {
                crc32 = crc32 >> 1;
            }
        }
```

```
            crcTable[tabIndx] = crc32;
        }

        return;
    }
```

B. RSA Public Key Cryptosystem:

File name: RSACryptoSys.cpp

```cpp
/*
    This function performs the following:
        1. Find 2 prime numbers, p and q
        2. Compute n and phi
        3. Find encryption and decryption keys, e and d
        4. Generate random message
        5. Encrypt the message
        6. Decrypt the message
        7. Compare the decrypted message with the original
           message.
*/
int32_t RSACryptoSys()
{
    int64_t p, q, temp;
    int64_t encriptKey;
    int64_t decriptKey;
    int64_t phi, nModulo;
    uint64_t orgMessage;
    uint64_t encMessage;
    uint64_t decMessage;

    p = findPrime(10, 10);
    while (p > 0x7FFFFFFF) // Limit p to 32-bit integer
    {
        p = findPrime(10, 10);
    }
    std::cout << "p = " << p << "\n";

    q = findPrime(10, 10);
    while (q > 0x7FFFFFFF) // Limit q to 32-bit integer
    {
        q = findPrime(10, 10);
    }
    while (q == p)      // q cannot be equal to p
    {
        q = findPrime(10, 10);
    }
    std::cout << "q = " << q << "\n";
```

```
temp = q;
nModulo = p * q;
 // Limit nModulo to be less than 0x7FFFFFFF
 // because the message encryption may overflow.
 // Find q again.
 while (nModulo > 0x7FFFFFFF)
{
    q = findPrime(10, 10);
     while (q == p)      // q cannot be equal to p
    {
        q = findPrime(10, 10);
    }
    nModulo = p * q;
}
 if (q != temp)
{
     std::cout << "q = " << q << "\n";
}
 std::cout << "nModulo = " << nModulo << "\n";

phi = (p - 1)*(q - 1);
 std::cout << "phi = " << phi << "\n";

 // Find decryption key which is greater than p and q,
 // and is smaller than phi.
decriptKey = findPrime(16, 16);
 while ((decriptKey <= p) || (decriptKey <= q) ||
        (decriptKey >= phi))
{
    decriptKey = findPrime(16, 16);
}
 std::cout << "decriptKey = " << decriptKey << "\n";

 // Find encryption key by Extended Euclidean Algorithm
encriptKey = ExtendedEuclidean(phi, decriptKey);
 std::cout << "encriptKey = " << encriptKey << "\n";

 // If encryption key is greater than decryption key,
 // swap encryption and decryption keys.
 if (encriptKey > decriptKey)
{
    temp = decriptKey;
    decriptKey = encriptKey;
    encriptKey = temp;
}
 std::cout << "decriptKey = " << decriptKey << "\n";
 std::cout << "encriptKey = " << encriptKey << "\n";
```

248

```cpp
    // Generate the message where 0 < orgMessage < (n - 1)
    orgMessage = nModulo - 10;
    std::cout << "orgMessage = " << orgMessage << "\n";

    encMessage = BinaryPowering(encriptKey, nModulo,
                                orgMessage);
    std::cout << "encMessage = " << encMessage << "\n";

    decMessage = BinaryPowering(decriptKey, nModulo,
                                encMessage);
    std::cout << "decMessage = " << decMessage << "\n";

    if (decMessage == orgMessage)
    {
        std::cout << "Decrypted msg matches original msg\n";
        return 0;
    }
    else
    {
        std::cout << "Decrypted message failed\n";
        return 1;
    }
}
```

File name: findPrime.cpp

```cpp
/*
    Find a prime number
    P = 1 + (2 ^ k) * d
    To prevent the operation from overflow (the maximum
    Number of 64 bits is (2 ^ 63 - 1). There is
    limitation for k and d.
*/
int64_t findPrime(
    int32_t kMaximum,
    int32_t dScale)
{
    int64_t ranNumK;
    int64_t ranNumD;
    int64_t primeNum;
    bool   foundPrime = false;
    bool   testAgain;
    int64_t x, y, m, md, j, temp;
    int32_t k;
    int32_t foundCount = 0;

    // Loop for finding a prime number
```

```
    while (foundPrime == false)
    {
        srand((uint32_t) time(NULL));
        ranNumK = rand();
        // Less than kMaximum
        ranNumK = ranNumK % kMaximum;
        while (ranNumK == 0)
        {
            ranNumK = rand();
            // Less than kMaximum
            ranNumK = ranNumK % kMaximum;
        }

        temp = ((int64_t) 1 << dScale);
        ranNumD = rand();
        ranNumD = ranNumD % temp;      // d % (2 ^ dScale)
        while (ranNumD == 0)
        {
            ranNumD = rand();
            ranNumD = ranNumD % temp;  // d % (2 ^ dScale)
        }

        if ((ranNumD & 0x1) == 0)
        {
            ranNumD += 1;  // make sure d is an odd number
        }

        primeNum = ((int64_t) 1 << ranNumK); // (2 ^ k)
        primeNum = primeNum * ranNumD;       // (2 ^ k) * d
        primeNum += 1;          // P = 1 + (2 ^ k) * d

        k = 0;
        testAgain = true;
        foundCount = 0;
        // Test the generated number for the primality
        // for 10 times
        while ((k < 10) && (testAgain == true))
        {
            x = rand();
            while ((x < 2) || (x > primeNum)) // 1 < x < P
            {
                x = rand();
            }

            j = 0;
            m = (int64_t) 1 << j;  // m = 2 ^ j
            md = m * ranNumD;      // md = m * d
            // y = (x ^ md) mod P
```

```
        y = BinaryPowering(md, primeNum, x);

          while (j < ranNumK)
        {
            if (((j == 0) && (y == 1)) || (y == (primeNum - 1)))
            {
                foundCount++; // Probably a prime number
                break;
            }
            else
            {
                // Not a prime number
                if ((j > 0) && (y == 1))
                {
                    testAgain = false;
                    break;
                }
            }

            ++j;
                // y = (y ^ 2) mod P
            y = BinaryPowering(2, primeNum, y);
        } // while (j < k)

          if (j == ranNumK)
        {
            testAgain = false;
            break;
        }
          k++;   // find new x
    } // while ((k < 10) && (testAgain == true))

    // After 10 times of possible primality, it
    // could be prime.
      if (foundCount == 10)
    {
        foundPrime = true;
    }
} // while (foundPrime == false)

    return primeNum;
}
```

File name: ExtendedEuclidean.cpp

```
/*
    Extended Euclidean Algorithm
*/
```

```
int64_t ExtendedEuclidean(
    int64_t phi,
    int64_t d)
{

    int64_t en;
    int64_t u1, u3, v1, v3;
    int64_t xn, y1, y3;

    u1 = 1;
    u3 = d;
    v1 = 0;
    v3 = phi;

    while (v3 != 0)
    {
        xn = u3 / v3;
        y1 = u1 - v1 * xn;
        y3 = u3 - v3 * xn;
        u1 = v1;
        u3 = v3;
        v1 = y1;
        v3 = y3;
    }
    if (u1 < 0)
    {
        en = u1 + phi;
    }
    else
    {
        en = u1;
    }

    return en;
}
```

File name: BinaryPowering.cpp

```
/*
    Binary Powering Algorithm
*/
uint64_t BinaryPowering(
    int64_t key,
    int64_t nmodulus,
    int64_t message)
{

    uint64_t criptMessage;
    int32_t firstMSB = 0;
```

```cpp
    uint64_t bitMask = 0x8000000000000000;

    // Find the msb of 1
    // Starting from msb down to lsb to find the
    // first bit of 1
    while (((bitMask & key) == 0) &&
            (firstMSB < (sizeof(int64_t) * 8)))
    {
        firstMSB++;
        bitMask = (bitMask >> 1);
    }

    // The value is 64 bits
    // Find the MSB bit number
    firstMSB = ((sizeof(int64_t) * 8) - 1) - firstMSB;

    criptMessage = 1;
    while (firstMSB >= 0)
    {
        // C = (C^2) mod n
        criptMessage = (criptMessage * criptMessage) %
                            nmodulus;
        // Start from the most significient bit
        if (bitMask & key)
        {
            // Set C = (M * C) mod n
            criptMessage = (message * criptMessage) %
                                nmodulus;
        }
        --firstMSB;
        // Next lower bit
        bitMask = (bitMask >> 1);
    }

    return criptMessage;
}
```

C. Advanced Encryption Standard (AES):

File name: AESAlgorithm.cpp

```cpp
// AESAlgorithm.cpp : This file contains the 'main' function.
// Program execution begins and ends there.
//

#include <iostream>
#include <stdlib.h>
#include <time.h>
#include <math.h>
```

```
#include "externs.h"

int main()
{
    uint8_t cypherKey[256/8];
    uint32_t keyByte;
    uint8_t fwdSbox[256], invSbox[256];
    uint8_t cypherText[128/8];
    uint32_t roundKeys[60];
    uint32_t cypherLen, indx, indx1, temp, errCount;
    uint32_t keyWords;      // Nk
    uint32_t blockSize;     // Nb
    uint32_t numRounds;     // Nr
    uint8_t* inputText, outputText[ROWLEN * COLLEN];
    //uint8_t greekText[] = "It is all Greek.";
    uint8_t inputBuff[128/8];

    srand((uint32_t)time(NULL));

    // Generate random text for encryption
    // Text length is always 16 bytes
    for (indx = 0; indx < 16; ++indx)
    {
        inputBuff[indx] = rand() % 0xFF;
          // Idle loop for rand() to generate different
        // result
        indx1 = 0;
          while (indx1 < 100)
        {
            ++indx1;
        }
    }
    inputText = inputBuff;

    cypherLen = 256;     // Cypher length
    std::cout << "Key length = " << cypherLen;
    std::cout << "-bit\n";

    if (cypherLen == 128)
    {
        keyWords = 4;
        blockSize = 4;
        numRounds = 10;
    }
    else if (cypherLen == 192)
    {
        keyWords = 6;
        blockSize = 4;
```

```cpp
        numRounds = 12;
    }
    else
    {
        keyWords = 8;
        blockSize = 4;
        numRounds = 14;
    }

    std::cout << "Generate SBoxes\n";
    GenerateSBoxes(fwdSbox, invSbox);
    std::cout << "\n";

    keyByte = cypherLen / 8;

    for (indx = 0; indx < keyByte; ++indx)
    {
        cypherKey[indx] = rand() % 0xFF;
        // Idle loop for rand() to generate different result
        indx1 = 0;
        while (indx1 < 100)
        {
            ++indx1;
        }
    }

    std::cout << "Key Expansion\n";
    KeyExpansion(cypherKey, roundKeys, keyWords, blockSize,
                 numRounds, fwdSbox);
    std::cout << "\n";

    std::cout << "Cypher key:\n";
    for (indx = 0; indx < (cypherLen / 8); ++indx)
    {
        temp = ((uint32_t) cypherKey[indx]) & 0xFF;
        std::cout << std::hex << "0x" << temp;
    }
    std::cout << "\n";
    std::cout << "\n";
    std::cout << "Input text:\n";
    for (indx = 0; indx < 16; ++indx)
    {
        temp = ((uint32_t)inputText[indx]) & 0xFF;
        std::cout << std::hex << "0x" << temp;
    }
    std::cout << "\n";
    std::cout << "\n";
```

```cpp
/* Encryption */
std::cout << "Encryption\n";
Encryption(inputText, cypherText, cypherLen,
        fwdSbox, roundKeys);

std::cout << "Input text:\n";
for (indx = 0; indx < 16; ++indx)
{
    temp = ((uint32_t) inputText[indx]) & 0xFF;
    std::cout << std::hex << " 0x" << temp;
}
std::cout << "\n";
std::cout << "\n";

std::cout << "Cyphered text:\n";
for (indx = 0; indx < 16; ++indx)
{
    temp = ((uint32_t) cypherText[indx]) & 0xFF;
    std::cout << std::hex << " 0x" << temp;
}
std::cout << "\n";
std::cout << "\n";

// Clear the input buffer for decryption
for (indx = 0; indx < 16; ++indx)
{
    outputText[indx] = 0;
}

std::cout << "Decryption\n";
Decryption(cypherText, outputText, cypherLen,
        invSbox, roundKeys);

std::cout << "Output text:\n";
errCount = 0;
for (indx = 0; indx < 16; ++indx)
{
    temp = ((uint32_t)outputText[indx]) & 0xFF;
    std::cout << std::hex << " 0x" << temp;
    if (outputText[indx] != inputText[indx])
    {
        ++errCount;
    }
}
std::cout << "\n";

if (errCount == 0)
```

```
    {
        std::cout << "\nMatch original msg. NO ERROR!\n";
    }
     else
    {
        std::cout << "With errors!!!\n";
    }
}
```

File name: AddRoundKey.cpp

```cpp
// AddRoundKey.cpp - Add round keys to the state array
//
#include "externs.h"

void AddRoundKey(
    uint8_t inputBuff[ROWLEN][COLLEN],
    uint8_t outputBuff[ROWLEN][COLLEN],
    uint32_t blockSize,
    uint32_t round,
    uint32_t roundKeys[])
{
    uint32_t rowIndx, colIndx;
    uint32_t keyIndx, keyWord;
    uint8_t byteKey[4], temp;

    for (colIndx = 0; colIndx < COLLEN; ++colIndx)
    {
        keyIndx = (blockSize * round) + colIndx;
        keyWord = roundKeys[keyIndx];
        byteKey[0] = (keyWord >> 24) & 0xFF;
        byteKey[1] = (keyWord >> 16) & 0xFF;
        byteKey[2] = (keyWord >> 8) & 0xFF;
        byteKey[3] = keyWord & 0xFF;

        for (rowIndx = 0; rowIndx < ROWLEN; ++rowIndx)
        {
            temp = inputBuff[rowIndx][colIndx];
            temp = temp ^ byteKey[rowIndx];
            outputBuff[rowIndx][colIndx] = temp;
        }
    }

    return;
}
```

File name: BuffsSwap.cpp

```cpp
// BuffsSwap.cpp - Swap input and output buffers
//
#include "externs.h"

void BuffsSwap(
    uint8_t inputBuff[ROWLEN][COLLEN],
    uint8_t outputBuff[ROWLEN][COLLEN])
{
    uint32_t rowIndx, colIndx;
    uint32_t temp;

    for (rowIndx = 0; rowIndx < ROWLEN; ++rowIndx)
    {
        for (colIndx = 0; colIndx < COLLEN; ++colIndx)
        {
            inputBuff[rowIndx][colIndx]
                = outputBuff[rowIndx][colIndx];
            outputBuff[rowIndx][colIndx] = 0;
        }
    }

    for (colIndx = 0; colIndx < COLLEN; ++colIndx)
    {
        for (rowIndx = 0; rowIndx < ROWLEN; ++rowIndx)
        {
            temp = inputBuff[rowIndx][colIndx];
            std::cout << std::hex << " " << temp;
        }
    }
    std::cout << "\n";

    return;
}
```

File name: Decryption.cpp

```cpp
// Decryption.cpp - Decrypt the cyphered text
//
#include "externs.h"

void Decryption(
    uint8_t cypherText[],
    uint8_t inputText[],
    uint32_t cypherLen,
    uint8_t invSbox[256],
    uint32_t roundKeys[])
{
```

```cpp
    uint8_t inputBuff[ROWLEN][COLLEN],
            outputBuff[ROWLEN][COLLEN];
    uint32_t rowIndx, colIndx, indx, roundIndx;
    uint32_t keyWords;      // Nk
    uint32_t blockSize;     // Nb
    uint32_t numRounds;     // Nr

    uint8_t invMixConst[ROWLEN][COLLEN] =
{{0x0e, 0x0b, 0x0d, 0x09},
  {0x09, 0x0e, 0x0b, 0x0d},
  {0x0d, 0x09, 0x0e, 0x0b},
  {0x0b, 0x0d, 0x09, 0x0e}};

 if (cypherLen == 128)
 {
     keyWords = 4;
     blockSize = 4;
     numRounds = 10;
 }
 else if (cypherLen == 192)
 {
     keyWords = 6;
     blockSize = 4;
     numRounds = 12;
 }
 else
 {
     keyWords = 8;
     blockSize = 4;
     numRounds = 14;
 }

indx = 0;
 for (colIndx = 0; colIndx < COLLEN; ++colIndx)
 {
     for (rowIndx = 0; rowIndx < ROWLEN; ++rowIndx)
     {
         inputBuff[rowIndx][colIndx] = cypherText[indx];
         outputBuff[rowIndx][colIndx] = 0;
         ++indx;
     }
 }

 std::cout << "\nAddRoundKey:\n";
AddRoundKey(inputBuff, outputBuff, blockSize,
            numRounds, roundKeys);
BuffsSwap(inputBuff, outputBuff);
```

```cpp
    for (roundIndx = (numRounds - 1); roundIndx >= 1;
         --roundIndx)
    {

        std::cout << "\nInvShiftRows:\n";
        InvShiftRows(inputBuff, outputBuff);
        BuffsSwap(inputBuff, outputBuff);

        std::cout << "\nInvSubBytes:\n";
        SubBytes(inputBuff, outputBuff, invSbox);
        BuffsSwap(inputBuff, outputBuff);

        std::cout << "\nAddRoundKey:\n";
        AddRoundKey(inputBuff, outputBuff, blockSize,
                    roundIndx, roundKeys);
        BuffsSwap(inputBuff, outputBuff);

        std::cout << "\nInvMixColumns:\n";
        MixColumns(inputBuff, outputBuff, invMixConst);
        BuffsSwap(inputBuff, outputBuff);
    }
    std::cout << "\nInvShiftRows:\n";
    InvShiftRows(inputBuff, outputBuff);
    BuffsSwap(inputBuff, outputBuff);

    std::cout << "\nInvSubBytes:\n";
    SubBytes(inputBuff, outputBuff, invSbox);
    BuffsSwap(inputBuff, outputBuff);

    std::cout << "\nAddRoundKey:\n";
    AddRoundKey(inputBuff, outputBuff, blockSize,
                roundIndx, roundKeys);

    indx = 0;
    for (colIndx = 0; colIndx < COLLEN; ++colIndx)
    {
        for (rowIndx = 0; rowIndx < ROWLEN; ++rowIndx)
        {
            inputText[indx] = outputBuff[rowIndx][colIndx];
            ++indx;
        }
    }

    return;
}
```

File name: Encryption.cpp

// Encryption.cpp - Encrypt the input buffer

```c
//
#include "externs.h"

void Encryption(
    uint8_t inputText[],
    uint8_t cypherText[],
    uint32_t cypherLen,
    uint8_t fwdSbox[256],
    uint32_t roundKeys[])
{
    uint8_t  inputBuff[ROWLEN][COLLEN],
             outputBuff[ROWLEN][COLLEN];
    uint32_t rowIndx, colIndx, indx, roundIndx;
    uint32_t keyWords;      // Nk
    uint32_t blockSize;     // Nb
    uint32_t numRounds;     // Nr

    uint8_t mixConst[ROWLEN][COLLEN] =
    {{02,03,01,01},
     {01,02,03,01},
     {01,01,02,03},
     {03,01,01,02}};

    if (cypherLen == 128)
    {
        keyWords = 4;
        blockSize = 4;
        numRounds = 10;
    }
    else if (cypherLen == 192)
    {
        keyWords = 6;
        blockSize = 4;
        numRounds = 12;
    }
    else
    {
        keyWords = 8;
        blockSize = 4;
        numRounds = 14;
    }

    indx = 0;
    for (colIndx = 0; colIndx < COLLEN; ++colIndx)
    {
        for (rowIndx = 0; rowIndx < ROWLEN; ++rowIndx)
        {
```

```
                inputBuff[rowIndx][colIndx] = inputText[indx];
                outputBuff[rowIndx][colIndx] = 0;
                ++indx;
            }
        }

    std::cout << "\nAddRoundKey:\n";
    AddRoundKey(inputBuff, outputBuff, blockSize, 0,
                    roundKeys);
    BuffsSwap(inputBuff, outputBuff);

    for (roundIndx = 1; roundIndx < numRounds; ++roundIndx)
    {
        std::cout << "\nSubBytes:\n";
        SubBytes(inputBuff, outputBuff, fwdSbox);
        BuffsSwap(inputBuff, outputBuff);

        std::cout << "\nShiftRows:\n";
        ShiftRows(inputBuff, outputBuff);
        BuffsSwap(inputBuff, outputBuff);

        std::cout << "\nMixColumns:\n";
        MixColumns(inputBuff, outputBuff, mixConst);
        BuffsSwap(inputBuff, outputBuff);

        std::cout << "\nAddRoundKey:\n";
        AddRoundKey(inputBuff, outputBuff, blockSize,
                        roundIndx, roundKeys);
        BuffsSwap(inputBuff, outputBuff);
    }

    std::cout << "\nSubBytes:\n";
    SubBytes(inputBuff, outputBuff, fwdSbox);
    BuffsSwap(inputBuff, outputBuff);

    std::cout << "\nShiftRows:\n";
    ShiftRows(inputBuff, outputBuff);
    BuffsSwap(inputBuff, outputBuff);

    std::cout << "\nAddRoundKey:\n";
    AddRoundKey(inputBuff, outputBuff, blockSize,
                    roundIndx, roundKeys);

    indx = 0;
    for (colIndx = 0; colIndx < COLLEN; ++colIndx)
    {
        for (rowIndx = 0; rowIndx < ROWLEN; ++rowIndx)
        {
            cypherText[indx] = outputBuff[rowIndx][colIndx];
```

```
            ++indx;
        }
    }

    return;
}
```

File name: GenerateSBoxes.cpp

```cpp
// GenerateSBoxes.cpp - Generate forward S-Box and
// inverse S-Box
//
#include "externs.h"

#define ROTLEFT(x,shift) ((uint8_t) (x << shift) |
                                (x >> (8 - shift)))

void GenerateSBoxes(
    uint8_t fwdsbox[256],
    uint8_t invsbox[256])
{
    uint32_t indx, mod;
    uint8_t  b, affx, fwdByte, invByte;
    uint32_t temp, temp2;

    /* 0 is a special case since it has no inverse */
    fwdsbox[0] = 0x63;
    invsbox[0x63] = 0;

    mod = 0x11B;
    for (indx = 1; indx < 256; ++indx)
    {
        // Forward substitution byte table
        // Use Extended Euclidean Algorithm to find the
        // multiplicative inverse
        b = (uint8_t) GF_xgcd(indx, mod);

        // Compute affine transformation
        affx = b^ROTLEFT(b, 4)^ROTLEFT(b, 3)^
                ROTLEFT(b, 2)^ROTLEFT(b, 1);

        fwdByte = affx ^ 0x63;
        fwdsbox[indx] = fwdByte;

        // Inverse substitution byte table
        // Compute the affine transformation
        affx = ROTLEFT(fwdByte, 1)^ROTLEFT(fwdByte, 3)^
                ROTLEFT(fwdByte, 6);
        temp = affx ^ 0x05;
```

```cpp
            // Find the multiplicative inverse
            invByte = (uint8_t) GF_xgcd(temp, mod);
            if (invByte == (uint8_t) indx)
            {
                    invsbox[fwdByte] = invByte;
            }
            else
            {
                    std::cout << "\nError: ";
                    std::cout << std::hex << " 0x" << indx;
                    std::cout << "\n";
            }
    }

    std::cout << "\n";

    std::cout << "\nForward SBox:\n";
    for (indx = 0; indx < 256; ++indx)
    {
        if ((indx & 0xF) == 0)
        {
                std::cout << "\n";
        }
        temp2 = fwdsbox[indx];
        std::cout << std::hex << " 0x" << temp2;
    }

    std::cout << "\n";

    std::cout << "\nInverse SBox:\n";
    for (indx = 0; indx < 256; ++indx)
    {
        if ((indx & 0xF) == 0)
        {
                std::cout << "\n";
        }
        temp2 = invsbox[indx];
        std::cout << std::hex << " 0x" << temp2;
    }

    return;
}
```

File name: GF_divide.cpp

```cpp
// GF_divide.cpp - Performs division in finite field
//
```

```c
#include "externs.h"

void GF_divide(
    int32_t divdend,
    int32_t divisor,
    int32_t* quotient,
    int32_t* remainder)
{
    int32_t indx, mask, bitdend, bitvisor, temp1, quot;

    mask = 0x80000000;
    indx = 31;
    while ((((divdend & mask) == 0) && (indx >= 0))
    {
        --indx;
        mask = mask >> 1;
    }
    bitdend = indx;

    mask = 0x80000000;
    indx = 31;
    while ((((divisor & mask) == 0) && (indx >= 0))
    {
        --indx;
        mask = mask >> 1;
    }
    bitvisor = indx;

    indx = bitdend - bitvisor;
    temp1 = divisor << indx;
    mask = 1 << bitdend;
    quot = 0;
    while (indx >= 0)
    {
        quot = quot << 1;
        if (divdend & mask)
        {
            quot = quot | 0x1;
            divdend = divdend ^ temp1;
        }
        temp1 = temp1 >> 1;
        mask = mask >> 1;
        --indx;
    }
    *remainder = divdend;
    *quotient = quot;

    return;
```

```
}
```

File name: GF_modMult.cpp

```cpp
// GF_modMult.cpp - Performs multiplication, and modulo
// in finite field
//
#include "externs.h"

uint8_t GF_modMult(
    uint32_t multcand,
    uint32_t multplier,
    uint32_t mod)
{
    uint32_t product = 0;
    int32_t quotient, remainder;

    // Polynomial multiplication
    product = GF_polyMult(multcand, multplier);

    // Divide by modulo (0x11B)
    GF_divide(product, mod, &quotient, &remainder);

    return (uint8_t) remainder;
}
```

File name: GF_polyMult.cpp

```cpp
// GF_polyMult.cpp - Performs polynomial multiplication
// in finite field
//
#include "externs.h"

int32_t GF_polyMult(
    int32_t multcand,
    int32_t multplier)
{
    int32_t indx, mask, bitcand, bitplier, product;

    mask = 0x80000000;
    indx = 31;
    while ((((multcand & mask) == 0) && (indx >= 0))
    {
        --indx;
        mask = mask >> 1;
    }
    bitcand = indx;

    mask = 0x80000000;
```

```
    indx = 31;
     while ((((multplier & mask) == 0) && (indx >= 0))
    {
        --indx;
        mask = mask >> 1;
    }
    bitplier = indx;

    product = 0;
    mask = 1 << bitplier;
     while (bitplier >= 0)
    {
        product = product << 1;
         if (multplier & mask)
        {
             product = product ^ multcand;
        }
        mask = mask >> 1;
        --bitplier;
    }

    return product;
}
```

File name: GF_xgcd.cpp

```
// GF_xgcd.cpp - Extended Euclidean Algorithm
// to find the multiplicative inverse in finite field
//
#include "externs.h"

int32_t GF_xgcd(
    int32_t num,
    int32_t mod)
{
    int32_t u1, u3, v1, v3, xn, y1, y3;
    int32_t quotient, remainder;
    int32_t temp1, temp3;
    int32_t multInv;

    u1 = 1;
    u3 = num;
    v1 = 0;
    v3 = mod;

    while (v3 != 0)
    {
        // xn = u3 / v3
```

```
            GF_divide(u3, v3, &quotient, &remainder);
            xn = quotient;
            temp1 = GF_polyMult(v1, xn);
              y1 = u1 ^ temp1;          // y1 = u1 - v1 * xn
            temp3 = GF_polyMult(v3, xn);
              y3 = u3 ^ temp3;          // y3 = u3 - v3 * xn

            u1 = v1;
            u3 = v3;
            v1 = y1;
            v3 = y3;
        }
        if (u1 < 0)
        {
            multInv = u1 ^ mod;
        }
        else
        {
            multInv = u1;
        }

        return multInv;
}
```

File name: InvShiftRows.cpp

```
// InvShiftRows.cpp - Perform inverse row shift
//
#include "externs.h"

void InvShiftRows(
    uint8_t inputBuff[ROWLEN][COLLEN],
    uint8_t outputBuff[ROWLEN][COLLEN])
{
    uint32_t rowIndx, colIndx, indx, temp;
    uint8_t inByte;

    for (rowIndx = 0; rowIndx < ROWLEN; ++rowIndx)
    {
        temp = COLLEN - rowIndx;
        for (colIndx = 0; colIndx < COLLEN; ++colIndx)
        {
            indx = (temp + colIndx) % COLLEN;
            inByte = inputBuff[rowIndx][indx];
            outputBuff[rowIndx][colIndx] = inByte;
        }
    }
```

```
        return;
}
```

File name: KeyExpansion.cpp

```cpp
// KeyExpansion.cpp - Perform expanding the round
// key schedule
//
#include <math.h>
#include "externs.h"

#define ROTWORD(x,shift) ((uint32_t) ((x) << (shift)) |
                          ((x) >> (32 - (shift))))
uint32_t SubWord(uint32_t inWord, uint8_t sbox[256]);

void KeyExpansion(
    uint8_t cypherKey[],
    uint32_t roundKeys[],
    uint32_t keyWords,      // Nk
    uint32_t blockSize,     // Nb
    uint32_t numRounds,     // Nr
    uint8_t sbox[256])
{
    uint32_t temp, wordCnt;
    uint32_t indx, rcon;

    indx = 0;
    // Generate the words from the cypher key
    while (indx < keyWords)
    {
        roundKeys[indx] =
            (cypherKey[indx*4] << 24) +
            (cypherKey[indx*4 + 1] << 16) +
            (cypherKey[indx*4 + 2] << 8) +
            (cypherKey[indx*4 + 3]);
        ++indx;
    }

    indx = keyWords;
    rcon = 0x01;
    // Calculate the length of the round key schedule
    wordCnt = blockSize * (numRounds + 1);
    while (indx < wordCnt)
    {
        temp = roundKeys[indx - 1];
        // If the key word is the first word of the
        // 4 round key words.
```

```
        if ((indx % keyWords) == 0)
        {
            temp = ROTWORD(temp, 8);
            temp = SubWord(temp, sbox);
          temp = temp ^ (rcon << 24);

          rcon = rcon << 1;
            if (rcon > 0x80)
            {
                rcon = rcon ^ 0x11B;
            }
        }
        else
        {
            // For 256-bit cypher key
            if ((keyWords > 6) && ((indx % keyWords) == 4))
            {
                temp = SubWord(temp, sbox);
            }
        }

        roundKeys[indx] = roundKeys[indx - keyWords] ^ temp;
        ++indx;
    }

    return;
}

uint32_t SubWord(uint32_t inWord, uint8_t sbox[256])
{
    uint32_t indx, tempWord, temp1, outWord, subByte;

    outWord = 0;
    tempWord = inWord;
    for (indx = 0; indx < 4; ++indx)
    {
        temp1 = tempWord & 0xFF;
        subByte = sbox[temp1];
        subByte = subByte << (indx * 8);
        outWord = outWord | subByte;
        tempWord = tempWord >> 8;
    }

    return outWord;
}
```

File name: MixColumns.cpp

```cpp
// MixColumns.cpp - Perform mixing columns
//
#include "externs.h"

void MixColumns(
    uint8_t inputBuff[ROWLEN][COLLEN],
    uint8_t outputBuff[ROWLEN][COLLEN],
    uint8_t mixConst[ROWLEN][COLLEN])
{
    uint32_t rowIndx, colIndx, indx;
    uint8_t  outByte, mixByte;
    uint8_t  colBytes[COLLEN], rowBytes[ROWLEN];

    for (colIndx = 0; colIndx < COLLEN; ++colIndx)
    {
        // Extract the column
        for (rowIndx = 0; rowIndx < ROWLEN; ++rowIndx)
        {
            colBytes[rowIndx] = inputBuff[rowIndx][colIndx];
        }

        for (rowIndx = 0; rowIndx < ROWLEN; ++rowIndx)
        {
            for (indx = 0; indx < COLLEN; ++indx)
            {
                // Extract row from mixConst
                mixByte = mixConst[rowIndx][indx];
                // Finite field multiplication
                rowBytes[indx] = GF_modMult((uint32_t) mixByte,
                                     (uint32_t) colBytes[indx],
                             0x11B);
            }
            outByte = rowBytes[0]^rowBytes[1]^rowBytes[2]^
                    rowBytes[3];
            outputBuff[rowIndx][colIndx] = outByte;
        }
    }

    return;
}
```

File name: ShiftRows.cpp

```cpp
// ShiftRows.cpp - Perform row shifting
//
#include "externs.h"
```

```
void ShiftRows(
    uint8_t inputBuff[ROWLEN][COLLEN],
    uint8_t outputBuff[ROWLEN][COLLEN])
{
    uint32_t rowIndx, colIndx, indx, temp;
    uint8_t inByte;

    for (rowIndx = 0; rowIndx < ROWLEN; ++rowIndx)
    {
        temp = COLLEN + rowIndx;
        for (colIndx = 0; colIndx < COLLEN; ++colIndx)
        {
            indx = (temp + colIndx) % COLLEN;
            inByte = inputBuff[rowIndx][indx];
            outputBuff[rowIndx][colIndx] = inByte;
        }
    }

    return;
}
```

File name: SubBytes.cpp

```
// SubBytes.cpp - Perform byte substitution
//
#include "externs.h"

void SubBytes(
    uint8_t inputBuff[ROWLEN][COLLEN],
    uint8_t outputBuff[ROWLEN][COLLEN],
    uint8_t sbox[256])
{
    uint32_t rowIndx, colIndx;
    uint8_t inByte, outByte;

    for (rowIndx = 0; rowIndx < ROWLEN; ++rowIndx)
    {
        for (colIndx = 0; colIndx < COLLEN; ++colIndx)
        {
            inByte = inputBuff[rowIndx][colIndx];
            outByte = sbox[inByte];
            outputBuff[rowIndx][colIndx] = outByte;
        }
    }

    return;
}
```

File name: externs.h

```
// externs.h - Common definitions
//
#include <iostream>
#include <stdlib.h>
#include <time.h>
#include <math.h>

#include <stdint.h>

#define ROWLEN   4
#define COLLEN   4

extern uint8_t fwdsbox[256], invsbox[256];

void GF_divide(int32_t divdend,
               int32_t divisor,
               int32_t* quotient,
               int32_t* remainder);
int32_t GF_polyMult(int32_t multcand,
                    int32_t multplier);
int32_t GF_xgcd(int32_t num, int32_t mod);
uint8_t GF_modMult(uint32_t multcand,
                   uint32_t multplier,
                   uint32_t mod);

void GenerateSBoxes(
    uint8_t fwdsbox[256],
    uint8_t invsbox[256]);

void SubBytes(
    uint8_t inputBuff[ROWLEN][COLLEN],
    uint8_t outputBuff[ROWLEN][COLLEN],
    uint8_t sbox[256]);

void ShiftRows(
    uint8_t inputBuff[ROWLEN][COLLEN],
    uint8_t outputBuff[ROWLEN][COLLEN]);

void MixColumns(
    uint8_t inputBuff[ROWLEN][COLLEN],
    uint8_t outputBuff[ROWLEN][COLLEN],
    uint8_t mixConst[ROWLEN][COLLEN]);

void KeyExpansion(
    uint8_t cypherKey[],
    uint32_t roundKeys[],
```

```
        uint32_t keyWords,      // Nk
        uint32_t blockSize,     // Nb
        uint32_t numRounds,     // Nr
        uint8_t sbox[256]);

    void AddRoundKey(
        uint8_t inputBuff[ROWLEN][COLLEN],
        uint8_t outputBuff[ROWLEN][COLLEN],
        uint32_t blockSize,
        uint32_t round,
        uint32_t roundKeys[]);

    void Encryption(
        uint8_t inputText[],
        uint8_t cypherText[],
        uint32_t cypherLen,
        uint8_t fwdSbox[256],
        uint32_t roundKeys[]);

    void BuffsSwap(
        uint8_t inputBuff[ROWLEN][COLLEN],
        uint8_t outputBuff[ROWLEN][COLLEN]);

    void Decryption(
        uint8_t cypherText[],
        uint8_t inputText[],
        uint32_t cypherLen,
        uint8_t invSbox[256],
        uint32_t roundKeys[]);

    void InvShiftRows(
        uint8_t inputBuff[ROWLEN][COLLEN],
        uint8_t outputBuff[ROWLEN][COLLEN]);
```

www.ingramcontent.com/pod-product-compliance
Lightning Source LLC
Chambersburg PA
CBHW080550060326
40689CB00021B/4808